TEACHING OF ENGLISH

TEACHING OF ENGLISH

RANJANA BANERJEE

RAJAT PUBLICATIONS
NEW DELHI - 110 002 (INDIA)

RAJAT PUBLICATIONS
4740/23, Ansari Road, Daryaganj
New Delhi- 110 002 (India)
Phones : +91-11-23267924, +91-9811484973
Email: rajat_publication@yahoo.com

Teaching of English

Edition 2026

ISBN 978-81-7880-320-3

[The responsibility for facts stated opinion expressed or conclusions reached and plagiarism, if any, in this volume is entirely that of the Editor. The publisher bears no responsibility for them whatsoever.]

PRINTED IN INDIA

Published by Mrs. Seema Wasan for **Rajat Publications**

Preface

With globalisation ruling the order of the day and increased exposure to and interaction with do different cultures and countries being inevitable English has become the primary choice as the global *lingua franca*. The relevance and importance of English cannot be denied by anyone, and importance of English cannot be denied by anyone, and the process of globalisation which shows no signs of relenting, would only make, English all the more indispensable in the changing world.

This book has been written to serve as a guide for teachers on not just teaching English as a necessary subject, but an interesting and fascinating area of study. The cultural and social significance of English lies in many aspects, chief among them being social interaction a love for literature enabling the study of other subjects in greater depth, etc., being the second language of most people in the world its pre-eminence is quite conspicuous and it hardly need be said that no sphere of activity today has been spared the influence of the English language in its functioning.

This book equips English teachers with a reliable guide on good teaching methodologies and practices, enabling them to infuse novel and innovative methods in the way they practice their professional retailing and discussing current trends and practices in English teaching, the book also brings under its preview a whole host of suggestions and advice for teachers which can prove to them of great use in making English teaching more existing and interesting. Rules of English communication grammar and vocabulary teaching however, are not the only parts of the contents of the book. English literature and its study has also been delivered into. To conclude the informative and relevant nature of this book should under if of high value of the reader.

Ranjana Banerjee

Contents

1

English—A Global Language

The global spread of English over the last 40 years is remarkable. It is unprecedented in several ways: by the increasing number of users of the language; by its depth of penetration into societies; by its range of functions. Worldwide over 1.4 billion people live in countries where English has official status. One out of five of the world's population speaks English with some degree of competence. Over 70% of the world's scientists read English. About 85% of the world's mail is written in English. And 90% of all information in the world's electronic retrieval systems is stored in English. By 2010, the number of people who speak English as a second or foreign language will exceed the number of native speakers. This trend will certainly affect the language.

English is used for more purposes than ever before. Vocabularies, grammatical forms, and ways of speaking and writing have emerged influenced by technological and scientific developments, economics and management, literature and entertainment genres. What began some 1,500 years ago as a rude language, originally spoken by obscure Germanic tribes who invaded England, now encompasses the globe. When Mexican pilots land their airplanes in France, they and the ground controllers use

English. When German physicists want to alert the international scientific community to new discoveries, they first publish their findings in English. When Indian executives conduct business with Scandinavian entrepreneurs, they negotiate in English. When pop singers write their songs, they often use lyrics or phrases in English. When demonstrators want to alert the world to their problems, they display signs in English.

Three factors continue to contribute to this spread of English:

— English usage in science, technology and commerce;

— the ability to incorporate vocabulary from other languages; and

— the acceptability of various English dialects.

In science, English replaced German after World War II. With this technical and scientific dominance came the beginning of overall linguistic dominance, first in Europe and then globally. Today, the information age has replaced the industrial age and has compressed time and distance. This is transforming world economies from industrial production to information-based goods and services. Ignoring geography and borders, the information revolution is redefining our world.

In less than 20 years, information processing, once limited to the printed word, has given way to computers and the Internet. Computer-mediated communication is closing the gap between spoken and written English. It encourages more informal conversational language and a tolerance for diversity and individual style, and has resulted in Internet English replacing the authority of language institutes and practices.

English, like many languages, uses a phonetic alphabet and fairly basic syntax. But most importantly, it has a large and extensive vocabulary, of which about 80% is foreign. Therefore, it has cognates from virtually every language in Europe and has borrowed and continues to borrow words from Spanish and French, Hebrew and Arabic, Hindi-Urdu and Bengali, Malay and Chinese, as well as languages from West Africa and Polynesia. This language characteristic makes it unique in history.

No English language central authority guards the purity of the language, therefore, many dialects have developed: American, British, Canadian, Indian, and Australian, to name a few. There is no standard pronunciation. But within this diversity is a unity of grammar and one set of core vocabulary. Thus, each country that speaks the language can inject aspects of its own culture into the usage and vocabulary. However, the future is unpredictable. There has never been a language so widely spread or spoken by so many people as English. So, there are no precedents to help us predict what happens to a language when it achieves genuine world status.

The world is in transition, and the English language will take new forms. The language and how it is used will change, reflecting patterns of contact with other languages and the changing communication needs of people. English is divesting itself of its political and cultural connotations as more people realize that English is not the property of only a few countries. Instead, it is a vehicle that is used globally and will lead to more opportunities. It belongs to whoever uses it for whatever purpose or need. One question that arises about the future role of the English language is whether a single world standard English will develop. This could result in a supranational variety that all people would have to learn.

The widespread use of English as a language of wider communication will continue to exert pressure toward global uniformity. This could result in declining standards, language changes, and the loss of geolinguistic diversity. On the other hand, because English is the vehicle for international communication and because it forms the basis for constructing cultural identities, many local varieties could instead develop. This trend may lead to fragmentation of the language and threaten the role of English as a lingua franca. However, there have always been major differences between varieties of English.

There is no reason to believe that any one other language will appear within the next 50 years to replace English. However, it is possible that English will not keep its monopoly in the 21st century. Rather, a small number of languages may form an oligopoly—each with a special area of influence. For example, Spanish is rising because of expanding trade and the increase of the Latino population in the United States. This could create a bilingual English-Spanish region.

A language shift, in which individuals change their linguistic allegiances, is another possibility. These shifts are slow and difficult to predict. But within the next 50 years, substantial language shifts could occur as economic development affects more countries. Because of these shifts in allegiance, more languages may disappear. Those remaining will rapidly get more native speakers. This includes English.

Internal migration and urbanization may restructure areas, thereby creating communities where English becomes the language of interethnic communication—a neutral language. Universities using English as the medium of instruction will expand and rapidly create a generation of middle-class professionals. Economic development will only increase the middle class, a group that is more likely to learn and use English in jobs.

While languages such as English, German, and French have been international languages because of their governments' political powers, this is less likely to be the case in the 21st century where economics and demographics will have more influence on languages.

Importance of Teaching English

English is not the most widely spoken language in the world in terms of the number of native speakers—there are many more Chinese speakers than native English speakers—but Chinese is spoken little outside of Chinese communities, so English is the most widespread language in the world. It is difficult to estimate exactly how many English speakers there are, but according to one estimate there are more than 350,000,000 native English speakers and more than 400,000,000 speakers of English as a second language (a language used in everyday life, even though it is not the native language) or foreign language (a language studied but not used much in everyday life).

However, even these numbers do not really indicate how important English is as a world language, because less than fifteen percent of the world population uses English. The importance of English is not just in how many people speak it but in what it is used for. English is the major language of news and information in the world. It is the language of business and government even in some countries where it is a minority language. It is the language of maritime communication and international air traffic control, and it is used even for internal air traffic control in countries where it is not a native language.

English as a First or Second Language

In some countries, English is the sole or dominant language. It has that role in the United Kingdom, the

United States, Canada, Australia, New Zealand, and Ireland. All of these countries are former British colonies. In other countries, English is widely used, particularly among people who have no other language in common, even though it is not the dominant language of the country. For example, English is widely used in Hong Kong, Singapore, Nigeria, the Philippines, and Malaysia. In such countries, it is often used as a means of communication between people who have different native languages.

English for News and Information

English is commonly used as a medium for the communication of information and news. Three quarters of all telex messages and telegrams are sent in English. Eighty percent of computer data are processed and stored in English. Much satellite communication is carried in English. Five thousand newspapers, more than half of the newspapers published in the world, are published in English. Even in many countries where English is a minority language, there is at least one newspaper in English. In India alone, there are three thousand magazines published in English. In many countries, television news is broadcast in English. Because of the power of television, demonstrators in every country use signs printed in English for the benefit of the international press.

English for Business and Diplomacy

English is a major language of international business, diplomacy, and science and the professions. It is the language that an Iranian businessman and a Indian businessman are likely to use to communicate. Important commodities such as silver, tin, and hard currency are traded in English. English is also an official language, or the official language, of many international organizations, including the United Nations and many professional organizations. It is frequently the language of international conferences, and it is the language of international athletics. Throughout the world, many professional papers are published in English. Even papers that are published in other languages often have abstracts in English.

English for Entertainment

Popular culture. Popular culture has also played an important part in spreading English. American and British popular music are heard all over the world. American movies are seen in almost every country. Books in English are available even in countries where few people actually use English. One reason that students give for learning English is to understand these songs, movies and books.

Travel. English is also very important for international travel. Much of the information countries disseminate about themselves outside of their borders is in English. English is spoken in large hotels and tourist attractions, at airports, and in shops that tourists frequent. There are newspapers printed in English, and TV news is available in English. Tours are almost always available in English. Even in countries where few people speak English on the street, people who work with tourists generally speak English. In some countries even drivers of buses or streetcars and sellers at newsstands speak English well.

In many former British colonies, English is still used in government and as a medium of communication among people who do not have another language in common. In some cases, it is a neutral language that is used to avoid giving any one indigenous language too much prestige. English is often used in India, because it is neutral. It is the language of government. People who speak English have a certain status in society. It is used for books, music and dance. In Singapore, English is a second language, but it is necessary for daily life. Many companies there use English. In addition, sixteen countries in Africa have retained English as the language of government. Now standard English is taught in schools in those countries, because it is necessary for careers.

English is also studied as a foreign language in countries where it is not generally used as a medium of communication. In China, English language lessons are popular TV programs. Two hundred fifty million Chinese—more than the population of the US—are learning English on TV. English is usually the first or most commonly taught foreign language in many countries, and people understand it a little at least.

Situation in India

Millions od Indians visit foreign countries each year, and more than one third visit English-speaking countries. Probably more than half of these people go abroad as part of a tour, and they do not speak English during the visit. They just see scenery, buildings, gardens, etc., eat in restaurants and stay at hotels. There is no contact with the people of the country. If they could speak English, at least they could talk with people in the countries where they visit. They could visit places on their own or take local tours. They can choose restaurants where they wanted to eat and shops where they wanted to buy things. They could get information though tourist information literature, newspapers, magazines, and TV programs.

Whenever we meet English-speaking people from various countries when we travel, they tell us that there are many Indian tourists in their cities or countries, but that the Indian tourists have difficulties speaking English. Nowadays many college graduates who work for large corporations will have opportunities to visit foreign countries on business or work in foreign countries. English is likely to be essential wherever they go, even if they are working in countries where English is not the dominant language.

India has achieved economic power and reputation for producing high quality manufactured goods. Many people throughout the world are interested in business, technology, and culture. However, there are not many foreign people who understand Indian languages. There are not many books, magazines, or computer sources to convey information on India. More and more information needs to be transmitted in English, so that many people in the world will know what is going on in India and can learn about Indian culture. We need more people who could convey information about India to the outside world.

More Indians attend international conferences and need to present papers and participate in discussions. Most international conferences are held in English. Many researchers in universities and companies attend international conferences to present the results of their research. Most presentations are in English. Their papers are also published in international journals, which are also in English. A great deal of information is available on the Internet. Most information on the Internet is in English, so if Indians want to take advantage of the many resources on the Internet, they need to be able to read English.

2

Curriculum Design

In formal education, a curriculum is the set of course and their content offers an institution such as a school or university. In some cases, a curriculum may be partially or entirely determined by an external body. The term curriculum may relate to the range of courses that students can select from but may also relate to a specific learning programme. In the latter context, the curriculum describes the collective teaching, learning and assessment materials that are available for that particular course.

A crucial part of the curriculum is the definition of the course objectives which are often expressed in terms of learning outcomes and normally includes the assessment strategy for the program. These learning outcomes are often grouped into units and the curriculum, therefore, comprises a collection of such units, each specialising on a specific part of the curriculum. So a typical curriculum would include units on communications, numeracy, information technology, inter-personal skills together with more specialised provision.

There are many possible starting points for curriculum design. For example:

1. Curriculum design can begin with the adaptation of an existing course, gradually reshaping it to become

quite different from what it was. This allows the course to be taught while curriculum design is going on.

2. Curriculum design can begin from an unorganized set of resources that are used, supplemented, adapted, or discarded as the design progresses. These resources can include course books, source books, teacher-made materials, and material from newspapers or magazines.

3. Curriculum design can begin from nothing except an idea in the mind of the designer.

Course design can be seen as a kind of writing activity and as such it can usefully be studied as a process. The typical subprocesses of the writing process (gathering ideas, ordering ideas, converting ideas to text, reviewing, editing) can be applied to course design, but it makes it easier to draw on current course design theory and practice if a different set of parts is used.

The model in Figure 1 illustrates the process of course design. The figure consists of three outside circles and a subdivided inner circle. Some course designers distinguish curriculum from syllabus.

In the model, both the outer circles and the inner circle make up the curriculum. The inner circle represents the syllabus. The outer circles (principles, environment, needs) represent practical and theoretical considerations that will guide the process of course production. There are many such issues to consider when designing a course. These include the learners' present knowledge and knowledge gaps, the resources available (including time), the skill of the teachers, the course designer's strengths and limitations, and principles of teaching and learning. If such factors are not considered, the course may be unsuited to the situation and learners and may be ineffective or inefficient in encouraging learning.

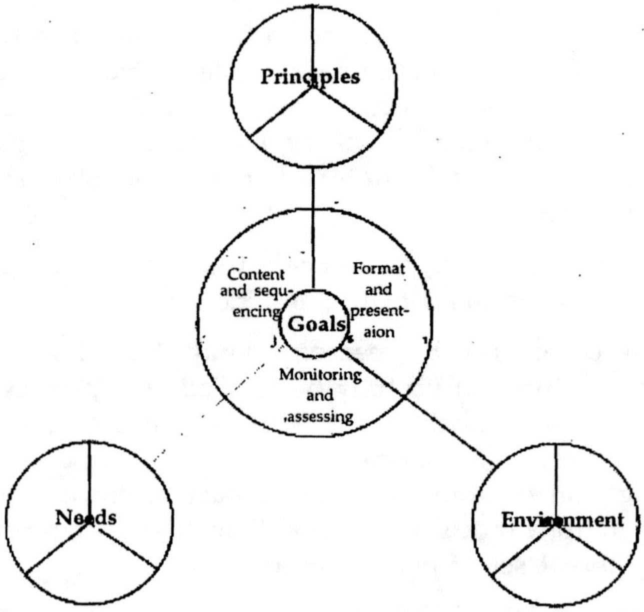

Figure 1. Process of course design

In the course design process, these factors are considered in three subprocesses: environment analysis, needs analysis, and the application of principles. The result of environment analysis is a ranked list of situational factors and a consideration of their effects on the design. The result of needs analysis is a realistic list of language ideas or skills to be achieved based on the present proficiency and future needs and wants of the learners. The application of principles first requires selecting the most important teaching and learning principles and then monitoring their application through the whole design process.

The inner circle has goals as its centre. This is meant to reflect the importance of having clear general goals for a course. The content and sequencing part of the inner circle represents the items to learn in a course and the order in which they occur. It also represents the ideas content if this is used as a vehicle rather than being a goal in itself. Language courses must give consideration to the language content of a course even if this is not presented in the course as a series of discrete items for study. Consideration of content makes sure that there is something useful for the learners to learn to advance their control of the language, that they are getting the best return for their effort, and that they are covering all the things they need to cover for a balanced knowledge of the language.

The format and presentation part of the inner circle represents the format of the lessons or units of the course, including the techniques and types of activities that will be used to foster learning. This is the part of the course that the learners are most aware of. It is important that it is guided by the best available principles of teaching and learning. The monitoring and assessment part of the inner circle represents the need to observe learning, test the results of learning, and provide feedback to the learners about their progress. It is often not a part of commercially designed courses. It provides information that can lead to changes in other parts of the course design process.

Now imagine a large circle drawn around the whole model. This large outer circle represents evaluation. Evaluation can involve looking at every aspect of a course to judge if the course is adequate and where it needs improvement. It is generally a neglected aspect of course design.

The shape of the model in Figure 1 makes it easy to remember. The three-part shape that appears in each of the outer circles also appears in the large inner circle and in the way the three outer circles connect to the inner circle. Let us now look at each of the sub-processes of course design, starting with the outer circles.

Environment Analysis

Environment analysis considers the situation in which the course will be used and determine how the course should take account of this context. One way of approaching environment analysis is to work from a list of questions which focus on the nature of the learners, the teachers, and the teaching situation. These include questions like, Do the learners share the same first language? How old are they? Do they have special purposes in learning English? Are they highly motivated? There is value in spending some time on these questions and their answers. Then choose three factors which will have the strongest effect on the design of your course, and rank them by importance.

Here are some of the top factors selected by several teachers designing different courses for different learners.

1. One teacher decided that the learners' lack of interest in learning English should be the major factor influencing course design. The learners were required to do an English course as part of their degree but received no credit for it. So the teacher's goal of making the course as interesting and motivating as possible guided the design of the course, particularly the format and presentation of lessons.

2. Another teacher decided that the learners' plan to move on to academic study in a university or technical institute should have the greatest effect on the design

of the English course. This had a far-reaching effect on the course's language items, the language skills it focused on, and its learning activities.

3. A third teacher decided that the externally designed and administered test at the end of the course should be the major consideration. This meant that the course book always had to make it obvious to the learners that the work they were doing was directly related to the test.

Here are some other factors that the teachers considered important:

— The small amount of time available for the course
— The large size of the classes
— The wide range of proficiency among the students
— The immediate survival needs of the learners
— The lack of appropriate reading materials
— The teachers' lack of experience and training
— The learners' use of the first language in the classroom
— The need for the learners to take more responsibility for their learning

Unsuccessful course designs often fail to take account of the environment questions. Here are some examples:

1. A communication-based course was deserted by its Vietnamese learners because they were not getting the grammar teaching that they expected. Instead they set up their own grammar-based course.

2. An English course for agricultural students had a simplified version of an English novel unrelated to agriculture as its main reading text. Some of the learners produced their own L1 translation of it, which

they copied and sold to other learners. They saw no value in coming to grips with its content through English.

3. One communicative course did not account for the learners' reluctance to be active participants.

Next to each important environment factor, note one or more effects. For example, the factor "the large size of the class" could have the following effects on the course design:

1. Incorporating a large amount of group work,
2. Using large-class techniques like text-recall activities, which work better the more learners there are, or
3. Training learners for independent work or individualized tasks.

The two main approaches to dealing with an environment are working within the constraint and working around the constraint. With a time constraint, for example, the goals can be adapted to suit the time available or extra time can be found by setting homework and other out-of-class activities. The importance of environment analysis is that it helps ensure that the course will be suitable, practical, and realistic.

NEEDS

Hutchinson and Waters make a useful division of learners' needs into necessities (what the learner has to know to function effectively), lacks (what the learner knows and does not know already), and wants (what the learners think they need). These are discovered by a variety of means: testing; questioning and interviewing; recalling previous performance; consulting employers, teachers and others involved; collecting data such as textbooks and manuals that the learners will have to read, and then analyzing them; and investigating the situations in which the learners will use the language. Ways of doing needs analysis can be evaluated by the same general criteria used to evaluate tests—reliability, validity, and practicality.

Necessities, lacks, and wants may all be compared against a list of learning goals for the course. An exception to this approach is to base the course on what the learners request, in which case the lists are created by the learners. This is effective if the learners have very clear purposes for learning English which they are aware of. For example, a course for immigrants who have been in the country a few months could very effectively be based on a list of things that they want to be able to do using English. One way of making needs analysis become a central, ongoing part of a course is to set up a negotiated syllabus. This means regularly involving the learners in decision making regarding the goals, content, presentation, and assessment of the course.

In its simplest form needs analysis should (1) assess how the learners will need to use the language after they leave the course, (2) measure the learners' present level of proficiency, and (3) ask the learners what they consider to be most important for them. The outcome should be a list of tasks or language features that can be the basis for the course.

PRINCIPLES

Research on language teaching and learning should be used to guide decisions on course design. There is considerable research on the nature of language and language acquisition which can guide the choice of what to teach and how to sequence it. There is also extensive research on how to encourage learning in general, and language learning in particular, which can be used to guide the class presentations. The principles derived from this research include the importance of repetition and thoughtful processing of material, the importance of taking account of individual differences and learning styles, and principles related to learner attitudes and motivation.

It is important for curriculum design to make the connection between the research and theory of language learning on the one hand and the practice of designing lessons and courses on the other. There is a tendency not to make this connection, with the result that curriculum design, and therefore learners, do not benefit from important research. A striking example of this is the failure of many courses to take account of research regarding the interference that occurs when semantically and formally related items (such as opposites, near—synonyms, and lexical sets) are presented together. In spite of the clear findings of this research, course books continue to present such topics as parts of the body; items in the kitchen; opposites such as *hot/cold, long/short, old/new*; numbers; days of the week; and articles of clothing in the same lesson.

Goals

The curriculum design model in Figure 1 has goals as its centre. This is because it is essential to decide why a course is being taught and what the learners need to get from it. Goals can be expressed in general terms initially and be given more detail when considering the content of the course. Here are some examples of goals set for language courses.

1. The aim of communicative teaching is to encourage students to exploit all the elements of the language that they know in order to make their meanings clear.

Students cannot be expected to master every aspect of the language before they are allowed to use it for communicative purposes.

2. The course aims to:

   (a) encourage students to communicate in a wide range of everyday situations,

   (b) sustain interest and motivation,

   (c) help students understand and formulate the grammatical rules of English,

   (d) develop students' receptive skills beyond those of their productive skills,

   (e) give students insights into daily life in Britain.

   (f) develop specific skills, including skills required for examination purposes, and

   (g) contribute to the students' personal, social and educational development.

Write a very short statement of the goals of the course to help clarify what the course is trying to achieve. Having a clear statement of goals is important for determining the content of the course, deciding on the focus in presentation, and guiding assessment. Learners can also benefit from being told about the goals.

Content and Sequencing

The content of language courses consists of the language items, ideas, skills, strategies, and tasks that meet the goals of the course. The unit of progression of a course is the language or content feature that represents movement or progress through the course. Some courses, for example, use grammar as the unit of progression, with each lesson dealing with a new grammatical feature. Progress through the course means increasing coverage of the grammatical features of the language. Other courses use tasks as the unit of progression. The tasks are chosen partly because of their resemblance to the language activities that learners will need to perform outside the course. Progress through the course is based on coverage of a range of language use tasks.

Even though the units of progression in a course might be tasks, topics, or themes, it is important for the course designer to check vocabulary, grammar, and discourse to make sure that important items are being covered and repeated. If the course designer does not check, learners may not learn items that are important for later use of the language. Learners also may not use items often enough to establish them in their minds.

One way to provide a systematic and well-researched basis for a course is to make use of frequency lists and other lists of language items or skills. These lists should be chosen and adapted as a result of the needs analysis in order to set the language learning content of the course. A list may be used as a way of checking or determining the content of a course, but this does not mean that the lessons have to consist of item-by-item teaching. A conversation course, for example, could be carefully planned to cover the important high-frequency vocabulary and structures, and still consist of a series of very free task-based conversation activities. Working from lists makes sure that what should be covered is covered and is not left to chance.

Typical lists include:

1. *Frequency-based vocabulary lists.* These are lists of words with indicators of their frequency of occurrence. Perhaps the best known is Michael West's. *General Service List of English Words* which contains 2,000 high

frequency word families. This is a good source for courses at the beginner and intermediate level. Other well-researched lists include *The Cambridge English Lexicon.*

2. *Frequency lists of verb forms and verb groups.* These contain items such as simple past, present continuous, verb + *to* + stem (where the stem is dominant) *going to* + stem, and *can* + stem (ability), along with information about their frequency of occurrence, mainly in written text. These lists can be found in George. The most striking feature of these lists is the very high frequency of a small number of items, such as the simple past and verb + *to* + stem, and the very low frequency of most of the items studied in the typical language classrooms. Comparison of beginners' books of published courses with these lists indicates that the mixture of high-frequency and low-frequency items in many course books could be considerably improved.

3. *Lists of functions and topics.* These lists are not frequency based, and as a result the selection of items must be based on perceived need, which is less reliable than frequency evidence.

4. *Lists of subskills and strategies.* These include the subskills of listening, speaking, reading and writing, and language coping and learning strategies.

5. *Lists of tasks, topics, and themes.* Course designers can refer to these lists but it is better for them to develop their own lists, taking account of the background of their learners and their needs.

Not only do lists check or determine the items that should be in the course, but they can be used to exclude items that should not be there, that is, those that are not in the list. The result of analyses based on lists is a set of language items that represent sensible and achievable goals for the course.

Needs analysis can play a major role in determining the content of courses, particularly for language items. As well as using needs analysis to set language goals, it is useful to decide the basis for the ideas content of the course.

An important decision to be made at this stage is the form the syllabus will take. Dubin and Olshtain describe several syllabus forms including linear, modular, cyclical, and matrix. Whatever form is chosen will have a marked effect on the opportunity for repetition of items to be learned. It can be argued that the first presentation of an item is not as important as the later repetitions of that item. This repetition is often neglected in courses, but it is crucial to learning. It is through repeated meetings that items are enriched and established.

Format and Presentation

The material in a course needs to be presented in a form that will help learning. The presentation will use suitable teaching techniques and procedures, and these need to be put together in lessons. Some lessons might consist of an unpredictable series of activities, while others might be based on a set format, where the same sequence of activities occurs in all or most of the lessons.

There are several advantages to having a set format for lessons. First, the lessons are easier to make, because each one does not have to be planned separately. It also makes the course easier to monitor, to check if all that should be included is there and that accepted principles are being followed. Finally, it makes the lessons easier to learn from, because the learners can predict what will occur and are soon familiar with the learning procedures required by different parts of the lesson.

The source material used for the lessons will affect the ease of making the lessons and of the possibility of future distribution or publication of the course. A shortcut is simply to take suitable material from other courses, adapting it as required, but this creates copyright problems.

Key principles need to be applied at this stage. Among the most important is the amount of time given to learning from listening and reading, learning from speaking and writing, direct study of language features, and fluency development.

The lesson format needs to be checked against the environment analysis of the course to make sure that the major environmental factors are being considered. Because course design is not a linear process, it may be necessary to alter the content or sequencing to suit the lesson format and to reorder the list of environmental factors. The lessons may require further adjustment at other stages of the course design. Perhaps the most difficult task at this stage is making sure that the learning goals of the course are met—that is, that the required language items are well represented and well presented in the course.

Monitoring and Assessment

The aims of course design are to make a course that has useful goals, achieves its goals, and does this in an efficient way. An important recurring part of the design process is to assess to what extent these goals are achieved.

Assessment generally involves the use of tests. An important distinction in testing is between proficiency tests, which measure what a learner knows, of the language, and achievement tests, which measure what has been learned from a particular course. Proficiency tests may be used to measure a learner's level of language knowledge before entering a course and after a course is completed. Achievement tests are closely related to a course, and the items in the tests are based on the content and learning goals of the course. Short-term achievement tests at the end of each lesson or group of lessons tell the teacher and learners how much has been learned. They can have a strong effect on motivation, on the speed of movement through the lessons, and on adapting and supplementing the course. Well-designed courses include short-term achievement tests in the curriculum design.

More comprehension achievement tests can be given at the end of a course and perhaps halfway through the course. The information gained from such tests can be useful in evaluating the course. Other kinds of tests include placement tests and diagnostic tests.

But testing is only one way of gaining information about the progress of learners and the effectiveness of the course. Other ways include observing and monitoring, using checklists and report forms, getting learners to keep diaries and learning logs, having learners collect samples of their work in folders, and asking them to talk about their learning. Curriculum design can plan for this kind of data gathering.

When improving an existing course, well-thought-out tests can be a useful starting point. The information gained from the tests can indicate areas in which the course needs to be improved.

EVALUATION

Information gained from assessment is a useful source of data about the effectiveness of a course, but it is only one of the sources of information that can contribute to the evaluation of a course. Evaluation tries to answer the question, "Is this a good course?" The range of meanings that can be attached to "good" depends on who is doing the evaluating and determines what sources of information are used to carry out an evaluation. Because there are so many sources, it is necessary to decide on an appropriate focus for evaluation.

A "good" course may be one that:

1. attracts a lot of students,
2. makes a lot of money,
3. satisfies the learners,
4. satisfies the teachers,
5. satisfies the sponsors,
6. helps learners gain high scores in an external test,
7. results in a lot of learning,
8. applies state-of-the-art knowledge about language teaching and learning,
9. is held in high regard by the local or international community, or
10. follows accepted principles of curriculum design.

An evaluation of a course can have many purposes, the main ones being to assess whether to continue or discontinue the course or to bring about improvements in the course. Responsible curriculum design includes ongoing evaluation of the course.

3

Teaching Techniques

Among the hundreds of English departments around the world there is a wide range of courses and degree structures. However, some features are regularly found. Early in your degree you will probably follow a set of courses/modules common to all the students on your degree scheme. Most of the courses will be taught using a relatively small number of teaching methods. This chapter explains some of the common methods of teaching and learning English.

Psycholinguistic Teaching Approach

The ability to carry out creative and effective communication is the main goal of all learners. Proficiency does not depend on linguistic knowledge. Language knowledge is secondary when compared to the functional ability of understanding and speaking, and reading and writing as a result. Therefore, while a structured syllabus can provide some basic language knowledge, it is only through the creative effort to communicate that complete communicative competence is acquired. The full process, from passive listening to understanding and from active thinking to speaking, needs to be thoroughly exercised. This can be achieved only through real human interaction.

Nobody fully acquires language ability with only books, tapes, VCRs, CD-ROMs or on-line exercises. Although such materials are helpful when designed according to contrastive linguistics, a brain needs another brain to interact with. Natural acquisition through real-life communicative experience can be complemented with audiolingual exercises and even with grammar study. Our unique teaching materials based on contrastive analysis play here an important role.

Curran believes that psychological counseling and foreign language tutoring are closely related. He advocates a unified concept of man and says that physical, intellectual, psychological and emotional factors can all influence language acquisition. Affection and an intimate relationship between the instructor and the learner, with both on the same level, provide the necessary framework. The instructor plays a non-authoritarian and non-directive role and activities are student-centered. The focus shifts from grammar and sentence formation to a deep sense of personal communication. When language is used to satisfy a strong desire to communicate, results can be impressive.

The counselor-teacher needs to try to build a personal relationship with the learner. Of course, this psychological involvement depends greatly on the student's personality. Therefore, the teacher must be constantly alert and able to recognize the communicative moments and opportunities and to explore them when they arise.

The key element of a psycholinguistic approach is the personal and intimate contact between learner and counselor. The learner's interests are explored and his own ideas are used as teaching materials. As in psychoanalysis, learner and counselor immerse in each other's mind. Instead of texts or tapes the thoughts of the learner, even the ones of neurotic origin, are discussed and brought to light in clear and appropriate language.

The goal is to increase the emotional load of the conversation, making the sessions more appealing and engaging. Resorting to the same resources used in psychoanalysis, the counselor-instructor plays the role of confidant and brings the conversation to the center of the learner's interest. The instructor adapts himself to the learner. If the learner is introverted, the instructor takes a leading role talking about himself, about his experience with the foreign culture, his difficulties and his weaknesses, opening his own heart, thus improving the mutual trust and creating an atmosphere for the learner to get ready. If the learner is extroverted, the instructor understands with empathy the learner's points of view encouraging him to express himself confidently. At this point the instructor helps the learner to reaffirm his opinions giving the precise language, just a little beyond the learner's capability. The learner will then see his convictions in convincing language, with good power of communication.

We do not emphasize error correction but communicative ability with beginners because psychological obstacles must be overcome before linguistic accuracy can be attained: Self-confidence and independence are the first steps. Still, linguistic forms like pronunciation and sentence patterns are not completely overlooked. These are discussed whenever necessary to address the learner's specific deviations. Again, the instructor needs to adjust his interventions to the learner. Introverts normally lack self-confidence and therefore should be less frequently interrupted and corrected than extroverts.

The Communicative-psychological approach is ideal for intermediate and advanced students and requires a skillful instructor. If not thoroughly bilingual, the person should be a native speaker of the target language with some command of the learners' native language. Besides the instructor's qualification the language therapy groups must be very small and homogeneous, with affinity between group members being very important.

Audiolingual Method

A. Important Concepts

1. Selection of materials — contrastive analysis

a. Major advocates and researchers in contrastive analysis: C.C. Fries and Robert Lado

b. Major claims:

The transfer claim: "Individuals tend to transfer the forms and meanings, and the distribution of forms and meanings of their native language and culture to the foreign languague and culture— both productively when attempting to speak the language and to act in the culture, and receptively when attempting to grasp and understand the language and the culture as practiced by natives."

The difficulty claim: "We assume that the student who comes in contact with a foreign language will find some features of it quite easy and others extremely difficult. Those elements that are similar to his native language will be simple for him, and those elements that are different will be difficult."

c. Method for doing contrastive analysis

— description (a formal description of the two languages involved)

— selection (certain areas or items of the two languages were chosen)

- — comparison (the identification of areas of difference and similarity)
- — prediction (determining which areas where likely to cause errors)

2. Teaching Process: Presentation - Practice - Application (Production)

Presentation— oral, dialogue, little explanation, L1 discouraged, errors corrected, accuracy emphasized, accurate repetition and memorization of the dialogue as goal of this stage;

Practice—pattern drills, mastery of the structure, fluency emphasized;

Application—use of the structure in different contexts;

3. Categorization of Drills: Mechanical, Meaningful, and Communicative drills

A mechanical drill is one where there is complete control over the student's response, and where comprehension is not required in order to produce a correct response.

Example: book —> this is a book. pen —> this is a pen.

A meaningful drill is one in which there is still control over the response, but understanding is required in order for the student to produce a correct response.

Example:

Teacher reads a sentence	Student choose a response
I'm hot.	I'll get you something to eat.
I'm cold.	I'll turn on the air conditioning.
I'm thirsty.	I'll get you something to drink.
I'm hungry.	I'll turn on the heater.

A communicative drill is one in which the type of response is controlled but the student provides his or her own content or information.

Teacher	Student completes cues
What time did you get up on Sunday?	I got up _____ .
What did you have for breakfast?	I had _____ .

B. Hands-on Activity

Dialogues are the basic form of instructional materials in the Audiolingual method. The dialogue serves three functions:

a) illustrates the target structure;

b) illustrates the situation the structure may be used; and

c) provides cultural information for language use wherever possible.

Write a dialogue of ten to fifteen exchanges that meets the following criteria:

1. It has a clear focus on an English sentence pattern you are trying to teach and the same sentence pattern is repeated several times in the dialogue.

2. It uses everyday vocabulary that is appropriate for beginning to intermediate level students.

3. There is no other sentence pattern or grammatical phenomenon that is new to students or more complicated than the sentence pattern you are trying to teach.

Then design three drills, one for each type discussed above, based on this dialogue for practicing the structure.

The following is an example:

— Hello Joy.

— Hello Daddy.

— How was your school today?

— It was all right.

— Do you have any homework today?

— Yes, the teacher asked us to copy some new words.

— Did she ask you to do any reading?

— No, she didn't ask us to do any reading. But she told us to write a story.

— Did she ask you to turn in the story tomorrow?

— No, she wanted us to turn in the story on Friday.

— What else did she want you to do?

— Nothing else. She wanted us to have fun.

— Do you want me to close the door.

— Yes, please.

A Mechanical drill

1. *Substitution/Replacement:*

He	me		to open the window.
They	wanted	him	to write a letter.
She	asked	them	to go home.
We	told	us	to shut the door.
I		her	to return the book.

2. *Transformation:*

He wanted me to open the window.	Did he want me to open the window? He didn't want me to open the window.

He asked me to return the book.
They wanted me to write a story.
We told him to buy a watch.
I asked her to visit me.

B. Meaningful Drill

Cues	Student
After I finished writing the letter,	I asked my mom to mail it.
When I got home,	my dad asked me to have a snack.

C. Communicative drill

Students answer the following questions based on real situations:

— What did your math teacher ask you to do this morning?

— What did I tell you to do before we began the new lesson?

— What do your parents often ask you to do on weekends?

Here is a list of structures you may use:

1. *passive voice:* The dog bit the child. The child was bitten by the dog.
2. *relative clause:* The man who is talking with my dad is my uncle.
3. *present continuous tense*: I am cleaning the window.
4. *simple future tense:* I will visit New York next summer.
5. *be going to:* I am going to play ping-pong tonight.
6. *plural form:* There are two books on the table.
7. *third person singular:* My dad goes to school everyday.
8. *present participle phrase modifying a noun:* Do you like the picture hanging on the wall?
9. *simple past tense:* I watched the game on Saturday.
10. *Adjective phrase used as adverbial of place*: I play volleyball near CDV every Friday.

Grammar Translation Method

The Grammar translation method, or classical method emerged when people of the western world wanted to learn "foreign" languages such as Latin and Greek. Its focus was on grammatical rules, the memorization of vocabulary and of various declensions and conjugations, translations of texts, doing written exercises.

A class working with the Grammar translation Method would look like that:

1. Classes are taught in the mother tongue, with little active use of the target language.
2. Much vocabulary is taught in the form of lists of isolated words.
3. Long elaborate explanations of the intricacies of grammar are given
4. Grammar provides the rule for putting words together, and instruction often focuses on the form and inflection of words.
5. Reading of difficult classical texts is begun early.
6. Little attention is paid to the content of texts, which are treated as exercises in grammatical analysis.

Direct Method

The basic premise of the Direct Method was that second language learning should be more like first language learning. The method would include lots of oral interaction, spontaneous use of language, no translation between first and second languages, and little or no analysis of grammar rules.

Here are the principles of the direct method:

1. Classroom instruction was conducted exclusively in the target language.
2. Only everyday vocabulary and sentences were taught.
3. Oral communication skills were built up in a carefully traded progression organized around questions-and-answer exchanges between teachers and students in small intensive classes.
4. Grammar was taught inductively
5. New teaching points were taught through modeling and practice
6. Concrete vocabulary was taught through demonstration, objects, pictures
7. Abstract vocabulary was taught through association of ideas.
8. Both speech and listening comprehension were taught
9. Correct pronunciation and grammar were emphasized.

Functional-notional Approach

This method of language teaching is categorized along with others under the rubric of a communicative approach. The method stresses a means of organizing a language syllabus. The emphasis is on breaking down the global concept of language into units of analysis in terms of communicative situations in which they are used.

Notions are meaning elements that may be expressed through nouns, pronouns, verbs, prepositions, conjunctions, adjectives or adverbs. The use of particular notions depends on three major factors:

a. the functions

b. the elements in the situation, and

c. the topic being discussed.

A situation may affect variations of language such as the use of dialects, the formality or informality of the language and the mode of expression. Situation includes the following elements:

a. The persons taking part in the speech act

b. The place where the conversation occurs

c. The time the speech act is taking place

d. The topic or activity that is being discussed

Exponents are the language utterances or statements that stem from the function, the situation and the topic.

Code is the shared language of a community of speakers.

Code-switching is a change or switch in code during the speech act, which many theorists believe is purposeful behavior to convey bonding, language prestige or other elements of interpersonal relations between the speakers.

Functional Categories of Language

Mary Finocchiaro has placed the functional categories under five headings as noted below: personal, interpersonal, directive, referential, and imaginative.

Personal = Clarifying or arranging one's ideas; expressing one's thoughts or feelings: love, joy, pleasure, happiness, surprise, likes, satisfaction, dislikes, disappointment, distress, pain, anger, anguish, fear, anxiety, sorrow, frustration, annoyance at missed opportunities, moral, intellectual and social concerns; and the everyday feelings of hunger, thirst, fatigue, sleepiness, cold, or warmth.

Interpersonal = Enabling us to establish and maintain desirable social and working relationships: Enabling us to establish and maintain desirable social and working relationships:

— greetings and leave takings

— introducing people to others

— identifying oneself to others

— expressing joy at another's success

— expressing concern for other people's welfare

— extending and accepting invitations

— refusing invitations politely or making alternative arrangements

— making appointments for meetings

— breaking appointments politely and arranging another mutually convenient time

— apologizing

— excusing oneself and accepting excuses for not meeting commitments

— indicating agreement or disagreement

— interrupting another speaker politely

— changing an embarrassing subject

— receiving visitors and paying visits to others

— offering food or drinks and accepting or declining politely

— sharing wishes, hopes, desires, problems

— making promises and committing oneself to some action

— complimenting someone

— making excuses

— expressing and acknowledging gratitude

Directive = Attempting to influence the actions of others; accepting or refusing direction:

— making suggestions in which the speaker is included

— making requests; making suggestions

— refusing to accept a suggestion or a request but offering an alternative

— persuading someone to change his point of view

— requesting and granting permission

— asking for help and responding to a plea for help

— forbidding someone to do something; issuing a command

— giving and responding to instructions

— warning someone

— discouraging someone from pursuing a course of action

— establishing guidelines and deadlines for the completion of actions

— asking for directions or instructions

Referential = talking or reporting about things, actions, events, or people in the environment in the past or in the future; talking about language (what is termed the metalinguistic function: = talking or reporting about things, actions, events, or people in the environment in the past or in the future; talking about language (what is termed the metalinguistic function:

— identifying items or people in the classroom, the school the home, the community

— asking for a description of someone or something

— defining something or a language item or asking for a definition

— paraphrasing, summarizing, or translating

— explaining or asking for explanations of how something works

— comparing or contrasting things

— discussing possibilities, probabilities, or capabilities of doing something

— requesting or reporting facts about events or actions

— evaluating the results of an action or event

Imaginative = Discussions involving elements of creativity and artistic expression

— discussing a poem, a story, a piece of music, a play, a painting, a film, a TV program, etc.

— expanding ideas suggested by other or by a piece of literature or reading material

— creating rhymes, poetry, stories or plays

— recombining familiar dialogs or passages creatively

— suggesting original beginnings or endings to dialogs or stories

— solving problems or mysteries.

Total Physical Response

James J. Asher defines the Total Physical Response (TPR) method as one that combines information and skills through the use of the kinesthetic sensory system. This combination of skills allows the student to assimilate information and skills at a rapid rate. As a result, this success leads to a high degree of motivation. The basic tenets are:

Understanding the spoken language before developing the skills of speaking. Imperatives are the main structures to transfer or communicate information. The student is not forced to speak, but is allowed an individual readiness period and allowed to spontaneously begin to speak when the student feels comfortable and confident in understanding and producing the utterances.

Technique

Step 1 The teacher says the commands as he himself performs the action.

Step 2 The teacher says the command as both the teacher and the students then perform the action.

Step 3 The teacher says the command but only students perform the action

Step 4 The teacher tells one student at a time to do commands

Step 5 The roles of teacher and student are reversed. Students give commands to teacher and to other students.

Step 6 The teacher and student allow for command expansion or produces new sentences.

Community Language Learning

This methodology is not based on the usual methods by which languages are taught. Rather the approach is patterned upon counseling techniques and adapted to the peculiar anxiety and threat as well as the personal and language problems a person encounters in the learning of foreign languages. Consequently, the learner is not thought of as a student but as a client. The native instructors of the language are not considered teachers but, rather are trained in counseling skills adapted to their roles as language counselors.

The language-counseling relationship begins with the client's linguistic confusion and conflict. The aim of the language counselor's skill is first to communicate an empathy for the client's threatened inadequate state and to aid him linguistically. Then slowly the teacher-counselor strives to enable him to arrive at his own increasingly independent language adequacy. This process is furthered by the language counselor's ability to establish a warm, understanding, and accepting relationship, thus becoming an "other-language self" for the client. The process involves five stages of adaptation:

Stage 1

The client is completely dependent on the language counselor.

1. First, he expresses only to the counselor and in English what he wishes to say to the group. Each group member overhears this English exchange but no other members of the group are involved in the interaction.
2. The counselor then reflects these ideas back to the client in the foreign language in a warm, accepting tone, in simple language in phrases of five or six words.
3. The client turns to the group and presents his ideas in the foreign language. He has the counselor's aid if he mispronounces or hesitates on a word or phrase. This is the client's maximum security stage.

Stage 2

1. Same as above.
2. The client turns and begins to speak the foreign language directly to the group.
3. The counselor aids only as the client hesitates or turns for help. These small independent steps are signs of positive confidence and hope.

Stage 3

1. The client speaks directly to the group in the foreign language. This presumes that the group has now acquired the ability to understand his simple phrases.
2. Same as 3 above. This presumes the client's greater confidence, independence, and proportionate insight into the relationship of phrases, grammar, and ideas. Translation is given only when a group member desires it.

Stage 4

1. The client is now speaking freely and complexly in the foreign language. Presumes group's understanding.
2. The counselor directly intervenes in grammatical error, mispronunciation, or where aid in complex expression is needed. The client is sufficiently secure to take correction.

Stage 5

1. Same as stage 4.
2. The counselor intervenes not only to offer correction but to add idioms and more elegant constructions.

3. At this stage the client can become counselor to the group in stages 1, 2, and 3.

AUDIOLINGUAL METHOD

This method is based on the principles of behavior psychology. It adapted many of the principles and procedures of the Direct Method, in part as a reaction to the lack of speaking skills of the Reading Approach.

New material is presented in the form of a dialogue. Based on the principle that language learning is habit formation, the method fosters dependence on mimicry, memorization of set phrases and over-learning. Structures are sequenced and taught one at a time. Structural patterns are taught using repetitive drills. Little or no grammatical explanations are provided; grammar is taught inductively.

Skills are sequenced: Listening, speaking, reading and writing are developed in order. Vocabulary is strictly limited and learned in context. Teaching points are determined by contrastive analysis between L1 and L2. There is abundant use of language laboratories, tapes and visual aids. There is an extended pre-reading period at the beginning of the course. Great importance is given to precise native-like pronunciation. Use of the mother tongue by the teacher is permitted, but discouraged among and by the students. Successful responses are reinforced; great care is taken to prevent learner errors. There is a tendency to focus on manipulation of the target language and to disregard content and meaning.

Hints for Using Audio-lingual Drills in L2 Teaching

1. The teacher must be careful to insure that all of the utterances which students will make are actually within the practiced pattern. For example, the use of the AUX verb have should not suddenly switch to have as a main verb.

2. Drills should be conducted as rapidly as possibly so as to insure automaticity and to establish a system.
3. Ignore all but gross errors of pronunciation when drilling for grammar practice.
4. Use of shortcuts to keep the pace o drills at a maximum. Use hand motions, signal cards, notes, etc. to cue response. You are a choir director.
5. Use normal English stress, intonation, and juncture patterns conscientiously.
6. Drill material should always be meaningful. If the content words are not known, teach their meanings.
7. Intersperse short periods of drill (about 10 minutes) with very brief alternative activities to avoid fatigue and boredom.
8. Introduce the drill in this way:
   a. Focus (by writing on the board, for example)
   b. Exemplify (by speaking model sentences)
   c. Explain (if a simple grammatical explanation is needed)
   d. Drill
9. Don't stand in one place; move about the room standing next to as many different students as possible to spot check their production. Thus you will know who to give more practice to during individual drilling.
10. Use the "backward buildup" technique for long and/ or difficult patterns.

    — tomorrow

    — in the cafeteria tomorrow

— will be eating in the cafeteria tomorrow

— those boys will be eating in the cafeteria tomorrow.

11. Arrange to present drills in the order of increasing complexity of student response. The question is: How much internal organization or decision making must the student do in order to make a response in this drill. Thus: imitation first, single-slot substitution next, then free response last.

Task-based Learning

Task-based learning is not entirely different from the aforementioned TTT, although this approach clearly takes into account the need for authentic communication. Typically there are three stages:

The Pre-task Phase

Before the task, the teacher explores the topic with the class. Useful (relevant) lexical items may be given. Also, the learners may be given further input, such as a recording of someone doing a similar task or part of an authentic text as a lead in. During the pre-task stage the learners will have their schemata activated, and given the opportunity to become personally involved in the lesson.

The Task Cycle

The task cycle can be broken down into three stages; task, in which the learners do the task; planning, when the learners prepare to report to the whole class (usually orally or in writing) how they did the task; and report, when the reports are presented to the class and results compared.

During the task, the teacher monitors and encourages all attempts at communication without correcting. Willis suggests that this harbours a free environment in whish learners are willing to experiment. At this stage in a PPP lesson the focus would be very much on accuracy, with all mistakes corrected. During the planning stage, the learners are aware that their output will be 'made public' and will consequently aim for accuracy. The role of the teacher here is therefore to provide assistance with regard to language advice. The teacher then chairs the report, and comments on the content. At this stage, the focus is on both fluency and accuracy. Also, the learners may hear a recording or read a text of a similar task, in order to compare how they did it.

Language Focus

The language focus consists of analysis and practice. In the analysis learners examine the recording or text for new lexical items or structures, which they then record. The teacher conducts a practice of the new items either during the analysis or after. The learners are given the opportunity to reflect on how they performed the task and on the new language they used in this final part of the lesson. Such a framework theoretically provides the learner with an opportunity to use the language they need for genuine communication.

A need to achieve the objectives of the task and report on it provide short-term motivation. Long-term motivation will be gained from successfully completing tasks. Bowen notes that the range of useable tasks offer a great deal of flexibility and should also lead to more motivating activities for learners. TBL also therefore accommodates different learning styles

There are clear instances in TBL in which the learner has the chance to privately practice the language, using it fluently, and then to publicly show other learners that they can use the language in a fluent and accurate manner.

There is no such opportunity or necessity for public performance in the other methodologies.

Task-based learning offers action and reflection. In contrast, PPP is relatively low in action and offers little if any chance for reflection as the language focus comes at the start of the lesson, and is entirely teacher generated. Learners who are used to a more traditional grammatical syllabus may find this approach difficult to come to terms with. This is primarily due to the apparent randomness of TBL, a criticism shared with TTT. Littlewood notes that one of the features of TBL that worries teachers is that it seems to have no place for the teaching of grammar. Nevertheless, Willis suggests there are two phases of TBL in which focus on form prove beneficial. Firstly, the planning stage between the private task and the public report promotes close attention to language form. Secondly, the language analysis activities provide a focus on form through consciousness-raising processes. To summarise, TBL does not mean 'forget the grammar'.

Utilising learner interaction as a teaching method is underused, mainly due to the fear of factors. However, the relevance of learner motivation and involvement cannot be overlooked. Learner-centred methods, such as TBL, draw on the learner's knowledge, and consequently materials are selected on the basis of both their needs and interests. Learning can be seen as a collaborative enterprise, in which there is a great deal of negotiation between the teacher and learner.

Stephen Krashen's Theory of Second Language Acquisition

Stephen Krashen (University of Southern California) is an expert in the field of linguistics, specializing in theories of language acquisition and development. Much of his recent research has involved the study of non-English and bilingual language acquisition. During the past 20 years, he has published well over 100 books and articles and has been invited to deliver over 300 lectures at universities throughout the United States and Canada.

Krashen's theory of second language acquisition consists of five main hypotheses:

— the Acquisition-Learning hypothesis,

— the Monitor hypothesis,

— the Natural Order hypothesis,

— the Input hypothesis,

— and the Affective Filter hypothesis.

The Acquisition-Learning distinction is the most fundamental of all the hypotheses in Krashen's theory and the most widely known among linguists and language practitioners.

According to Krashen there are two independent systems of second language performance: 'the acquired system' and 'the learned system'. The 'acquired system' or 'acquisition' is the product of a subconscious process very similar to the process children undergo when they acquire their first language. It requires meaningful interaction in the target language - natural communication - in which speakers are concentrated not in the form of their utterances, but in the communicative act.

The 'learned system' or 'learning' is the product of formal instruction and it comprises a conscious process which results in conscious knowledge 'about' the language, for example knowledge of grammar rules. According to Krashen 'learning' is less important than 'acquisition'.

The Monitor hypothesis explains the relationship between acquisition and learning and defines the influence of the latter on the former. The monitoring function is the practical result of the learned grammar. According to Krashen, the acquisition system is the utterance initiator, while the learning system performs the role of the 'monitor' or the 'editor'. The 'monitor' acts in a planning, editing and correcting function when three specific conditions are met: that is, the second language learner has sufficient time at his/her disposal, he/she focuses on form or thinks about correctness, and he/she knows the rule.

It appears that the role of conscious learning is somewhat limited in second language performance. According to Krashen, the role of the monitor is - or should be - minor, being used only to correct deviations from 'normal' speech and to give speech a more 'polished' appearance.

Krashen also suggests that there is individual variation among language learners with regard to 'monitor' use. He distinguishes those learners that use the 'monitor' all the time (over-users); those learners who have not learned or who prefer not to use their conscious knowledge (under-users); and those learners that use the 'monitor' appropriately (optimal users). An evaluation of the person's psychological profile can help to determine to what group they belong. Usually extroverts are under-users, while introverts and perfectionists are over-users. Lack of self-confidence is frequently related to the over-use of the 'monitor'

The Natural Order hypothesis is based on research findings which suggested that the acquisition of grammatical structures follows a 'natural order' which is predictable. For a given language, some grammatical structures tend to be acquired early while others late. This order seemed to be independent of the learners' age, L1 background, conditions of exposure, and although the agreement between individual acquirers was not always 100% in the studies, there were statistically significant similarities that reinforced the existence of a Natural Order of language acquisition. Krashen however points out that the implication of the natural order hypothesis is not that a language program syllabus should be based on the order found in the studies. In fact, he rejects grammatical sequencing when the goal is language acquisition.

The Input hypothesis is Krashen's attempt to explain how the learner acquires a second language. In other words, this hypothesis is Krashen's explanation of how second language acquisition takes place. So, the Input hypothesis is only concerned with 'acquisition', not 'learning'. According to this hypothesis, the learner improves and progresses along the 'natural order' when he/she receives second language 'input' that is one step beyond his/her current stage of linguistic competence. For example, if a learner is at a stage 'i', then acquisition takes place when he/she is exposed to 'Comprehensible Input' that belongs to level 'i + 1'. Since not all of the learners can be at the same level of linguistic competence at the same time, Krashen suggests that natural communicative input is the key to designing a syllabus, ensuring in this way that each learner will receive some 'i + 1' input that is appropriate for his/her current stage of linguistic competence.

Finally, the fifth hypothesis, the Affective Filter hypothesis, embodies Krashen's view that a number of 'affective variables' play a facilitative, but non-causal, role in second language acquisition. These variables include: motivation, self-confidence and anxiety. Krashen claims that learners with high motivation, self-confidence, a good self-image, and a low level of anxiety are better equipped for success in second language acquisition. Low motivation, low self-esteem, and debilitating anxiety can combine to 'raise' the affective filter and form a 'mental block' that prevents comprehensible input from being used for acquisition. In other words, when the filter is 'up' it impedes language acquisition. On the other hand, positive affect is necessary, but not sufficient on its own, for acquisition to take place.

Role of Grammar in Krashen's View

According to Krashen, the study of the structure of the language can have general educational advantages and values that high schools and colleges may want to include in their language programs. It should be clear, however, that examining irregularity, formulating rules and teaching complex facts about the target language is not language teaching, but rather is "language appreciation" or linguistics.

The only instance in which the teaching of grammar can result in language acquisition (and proficiency) is when the students are interested in the subject and the target language is used as a medium of instruction. Very often, when this occurs, both teachers and students are convinced that the study of formal grammar is essential for second language acquisition, and the teacher is skillful enough to present explanations in the target language so that the students understand. In other words, the teacher talk meets the requirements for comprehensible input and perhaps with the students' participation the classroom becomes an environment suitable for acquisition. Also, the filter is low in regard to the language of explanation, as the students' conscious efforts are usually on the subject matter, on what is being talked about, and not the medium.

This is a subtle point. In effect, both teachers and students are deceiving themselves. They believe that it is the subject matter itself, the study of grammar, that is responsible for the students' progress, but in reality their progress is coming from the medium and not the message. Any subject matter that held their interest would do just as well.

THE SILENT WAY

The idea that a foreign language could be learned by memorising lists of vocabulary and grammar rules and by continual reference to one's native tongue has been rejected by most teachers of foreign languages today. Of the many alternative methods in use now, most have common basic elements: the learning of phrases and sentences instead of single words, the infrequent use of the native tongue, the emphasis on the spoken language, etc., but all still rely on memory as the key to mastery and include a variety of tools to aid memory, including video and audio tapes, drills and exercises. At the same time many of these new methods claim to teach the foreign language in imitation or simulation of the way a baby learns his native tongue. These approaches overlook some very basic truths. If one considers speaking one's native tongue it becomes immediately clear that one does not remember it, one uses it. Situations trigger verbal responses. It is also evident that memory is one of our weakest faculties and therefore makes a poor basis for learning.

In all languages there are two kinds of words; those which can be simply substituted one for another from one language to the next, and those which cannot be dealt with in this way. The first group includes all names of objects that belong to the environments of the people using the language in question. Most nouns are in this category. These words can be matched in a one-to-one correspondence and we could conceive of them as being in vocabularies only requiring either to be recalled or looked-up.

The second category of words is the one that generates the problems in language learning. Since it is not possible to resort to a one-to-one correspondence, the only way open is to reach the area of meaning that the words cover, and find in oneself whether this is a new experience which yields something of the spirit of the language, or whether there is an equivalent experience in one's own language but expressed differently. To make sense of an original text written by a native, one needs much more than a morphological knowledge of the language and the possession of a set of equivalents.

If we consider the problems met in the acquisition of the second group of words mentioned above, it seems obvious that recourse to one's native tongue is not helpful, and the language ought to be blocked. But the acquisition of the mother tongue brings with it an awareness of what language is and it is this that must be retained; it is by keeping in touch with this awareness that a student who has already mastered his first language is in an appreciably stronger position when it comes to tackling a second.

Awareness of what language is includes the use of non-verbal components of language: melody, rhythm, intonation, breathing, inflection, etc. We could add to this awareness connected to the reading of a language: the conventions of writing, the combinations of letters to form the signs of different sounds and the possibility of one sound being represented by more than one combination.

Thus there is no chance to present to a learner of a foreign language any situation comparable to that which he has faced as a baby. The presentation of a foreign language in a classroom is far from natural and it can only be learned in school by artificial methods constructed for the purpose. In a classroom a teacher is there to present what is to be learned in a highly controlled way, which is quite unlike the situation for babies, who are subjected to a flow of words knitted together by the sustaining meaning, and coming from the source as a whole. People in contact with babies do not take special care when addressing them: they use the language which is available to them to say all they wish to say as completely as when talking among themselves.

Our proposal is to apply an artificial and for some purposes a strictly controlled approach, using materials constructed for this purpose. We will meet our students as people who already own much of what is needed to acquire a language and who have shown by the acquisition of their native tongue that they are endowed with mental powers that are, to say the least, sizeable. We make a start with the vocabulary of the second group of words, which we call the functional vocabulary. By using a number of small coloured rods, the teacher creates simple linguistic situations which are totally under her control. The situations can be very simple. They can be gradually made more complex as progress is made. The rods are used here to provide the support of perception and action to the intellectual guess of what the noises mean, thus bringing in the arsenal of criteria already developed and automatic in one's use of one's native tongue.

The structure used above can be transformed immediately into any description involving spatial relations and comparisons by the substitution of other nouns and adjectives. The rods are portable and easy to manipulate. They have qualities of colour, size and number. They can be used to build houses, furniture, clocks, etc., to represent people, family trees and with the help of imagination, anything else needed and not available in a classroom. Unlike pictures, they create situations which are not static, allowing for a sequence of events to take place and thus be spoken about, respecting the place of time in language.

Once some vocabulary has been met, reading is introduced through the wall charts. These present in a clear, logical and simple form what is in fact a highly complex analysis of the structure of words and their pronunciation. The vocabulary provided on the word charts is adequate for a multitude of different situations because the charts give a large proportion of the most common and useful words in each of the languages concerned. This enables a wide range of different sentences to be produced by selecting with a pointer particular words in appropriate sentences. The colouring principle, once discovered or explained, practically ensures correct pronunciation without need for memorising the code. Students do not ever write in colour. The correct use of the pointer with the charts will indicate phrasing, stress, speed, rhythm and intonation.

The various language fidels are comprehensive sound-sign analyses. Divided horizontally into two sections, the upper part concerned with vowels, the lower with consonants, these tables list in columns the different ways of spelling the various sounds in a particular language. Once the functional vocabulary has been mastered the fidels provide the opportunity for numerous games which allow the study of the complete set of signs and sounds of the language. The wall pictures present drawings of everyday life and are for the expansion of vocabulary. They stimulate the introduction of nouns and new verbs which form part of the day-to-day vocabulary of the people speaking the language. This vocabulary which we call semi-luxury, includes food, travel, family life, outings, etc. There are accompanying worksheets which require a variety of sensitivities from the learner.

Procedures

This method begins by using a set of colored rods and verbal commands in order to achieve the following:

To avoid the use of the vernacular. To create simple linguistic situations that remain under the complete control of the teacher To pass on to the learners the responsibility for the utterances of the descriptions of the objects shown or the actions performed. To let the teacher concentrate on what the students say and how they are saying it, drawing their attention to the differences in pronunciation and the flow of words. To generate a serious game-like situation in which the rules are implicitly agreed upon by giving meaning to the gestures of the teacher and his mime. To permit almost from the start a switch from the lone voice of the teacher using the foreign language to a number of voices using it. This introduces components of pitch, timbre and intensity that will constantly reduce the impact of one voice and hence reduce imitation and encourage personal production of one's own brand of the sounds.

To provide the support of perception and action to the intellectual guess of what the noises mean, thus bring in the arsenal of the usual criteria of experience already developed and automatic in one's use of the mother tongue. To provide a duration of spontaneous speech upon which the teacher and the students can work to obtain a similarity of melody to the one heard, thus providing melodic integrative schemata from the start.

4

Teaching English at Post-Primary Level

The school timetable is the first source of information on the most basic aspect of provision for English, namely the number and distribution of English lessons for each class. The optimal situation is for students to have an English lesson on each of the five days of the week, to enable them to develop the necessary skills and competences and to provide them with regular reinforcement of these.

Concurrent timetabling for English involves the timetabling of English lessons at the same time for all classes in a year group. It is a valuable practice, as it not only facilitates the movement of students between levels but also creates opportunities for interclass and whole-year activities and for team teaching. However, concurrence makes considerable demands on timetabling and should therefore be used to the full.

The concurrent timetabling of English within fifth and sixth year was widespread but was often used only to allow movement between levels. All the uses of concurrence mentioned above apply equally to the junior cycle, yet concurrence was rare in first year and occurred in fewer than half the schools in second and third year. Concurrence is also recommended in transition year, as it opens up opportunities for whole-year activities and the team-teaching of modules. It should be noted that concurrence is unlikely to be exploited fully unless it is the focus of careful collaborative planning.

Most schools reported that teachers were deployed across a range of programmes and levels. However, it was clear that in many instances teachers were teaching in the junior cycle but not the senior cycle, or vice versa, or took only higher-level or only ordinary-level classes. Good deployment of teachers should serve to broaden and deepen the pool of expertise and experience within the subject department and should offer teachers opportunities and challenges to extend their range. Therefore, a well-planned rotation of teachers so that they encounter students across the spectrum of years, levels and programmes represents best practice and is strongly recommended by the inspectors of English.

It follows from this that teachers of English should have a substantial timetable commitment to the subject. However, in a significant number of schools some of those teaching English took only one class group and therefore had a teaching load for English of no more than four or five lessons per week. Timetabling constraints, staff changes and the demands made by teachers' other subjects inevitably have a bearing on deployment. Nonetheless, timetabling teachers to take English with only one class group should be avoided where possible.

The inspectors particularly noted the high incidence of this practice in first-year classes as a cause for concern. Given the significance of first year for the teaching and learning of essential skills, it is recommended that teachers taking first-years for English also take other year groups and have a broad involvement with the subject. Continuity of teacher from one year to the next within a cycle or programme is generally desirable and should be kept in mind in planning both at the wholeschool level and the subject department level.

Schools throughout the country have seen an increase in the numbers of international students who are entitled to language support. The aim of language support is to provide specific tuition in English for speakers of other languages. While a number of schools were offering structured language support to international students through teachers who have some training in the area, there was a lack of coherence in the provision and delivery of this support in many other instances.

All schools with students requiring language support should liaise with Integrate Ireland Language and Training (IILT), which has a specific remit to assist language-support teachers through the provision of training and resource materials. School managements should ensure that there is as much continuity as possible in the deployment of language-support teachers, so that skills developed through training are used effectively.

Mixed ability is a method of class formation that entails the distribution of students of all levels of ability across all class groups. More than half the schools used this method for first-year class formation, and of these the majority continued mixed ability into second year. Where a school used mixed ability in first year and not in second year the usual reason was that students were being set into higher-level and ordinary-level groups at that point. It is recommended that decisions in relation to level, and the rearranging of class groups that may arise from these decisions, be deferred until the end of second year at least. This policy gives more time to students when they are going through an important phase of development and encourages them to have the highest realistic expectations.

In banding, a number of class groups are formed within ability bands. Banding operated in the junior cycle in a minority of schools, most of which had a large enrolment with a very wide spread of ability. A number of reports noted the effective use of banding to support both very able and very weak students. Streaming, in which students are placed in a particular ability group for all subjects, was observed in a few schools in the junior cycle. The reports on these schools recommend a move to banding for schools with a large enrolment or to mixed ability for smaller schools, given the negative effect of streaming on students' expectations and development of potential.

In accordance with the spirit and the aims of the Transition Year programme, all transition-year classes should be of mixed ability, and this practice was followed in almost all the schools offering the programme. In most schools, fifth-year and sixth-year classes were set for English and were usually designated as higher and ordinary level, though there were also mixed-level classes.

Traditionally, English has been regarded as a "resource-light" subject, which can be taught anywhere. Given syllabus changes and the introduction of new programmes, this is no longer a tenable view, if indeed it ever was.

There are certain basic requirements for all rooms in which English is taught:

— a good-sized board with a high-quality writing surface

— students' seating sufficiently flexible to facilitate pair and group work

— display spaces for students' work and for relevant illustrative material.

A number of the classrooms visited fell below even this basic level of provision; yet the classroom in which English is taught should be a resource in itself, an environment rich in print and also conducive to the study of the spoken word and visual texts. Therefore, the schools that exemplified best practice were those where, in the English classrooms,

— books, including dictionaries, were on display and in use

— audio equipment was available and used appropriately

— a television of adequate screen size, with video or DVD player, was available and used appropriately.

The variety of functions and the good picture quality available with DVD make this a more useful format for film in the classroom. Where audiovisual equipment is shared and centrally stored, an agreed booking procedure should be followed.

The majority of schools operate teacher-based rooms. In the schools in this sample that had teacher based rooms, most teachers of English had their own rooms, with the general exception of newer teachers or those not on full hours. It would be helpful if teachers without a room of their own could take their classes in the same room every day, in order to develop it as a resource and to establish a routine for access to materials and equipment. Shared resources for the English department should be kept in an accessible storage area or room.

Although the inspectors of English have seen some very good libraries in schools in all sectors, a significant minority of schools have no library, and fewer than a third of those that have are making optimal use of it. Where rooms that were once libraries are now being used for other purposes, the school management usually cited under-use of the library as a reason for the change. Schools with a successful library had in common:

— a commitment to the library on the part of the management and members of staff

— a designated member of staff, teaching or non-teaching, who acted as librarian

— provision for the updating of stock and the maintenance of a wide selection of books

— the promotion of the library as a source of reading for pleasure

— the promotion of the library in all subject areas as a place for research

— good opportunities for students to have access to the library

— a number of computers with internet access in the library.

Book boxes and classroom libraries were used to foster the reading habit in a number of schools, especially where there was no library or where students' reading needed particular encouragement. Even where school libraries are flourishing, such initiatives extend the reading opportunities for students.

In addition, these collections of books can be tailored to the needs of particular classes. Teachers are commended for the efforts they make to instil a love of reading, and school managements should be active in supporting their efforts.

The availability of information and communications technology (ICT) in schools has had a discernible impact on how teachers research and prepare lessons and materials. Worksheets, templates and resource notes are increasingly produced on computer, aiding legibility and ease of use. Teachers are also increasingly using the internet for their own research and for material to download for class use. Guiding students to useful web sites and instructing them in the appropriate use of material obtained on the internet should now be seen as part of the teacher's role. In particular, issues of plagiarism and the proper acknowledgement of sources should be dealt with in the school's policy on acceptable internet use.

While only a small number of schools had an annual budget for English, most teachers reported positive responses to requests for resources. In a significant number of instances, teachers were purchasing resources themselves. While a certain amount of individual purchasing may be inevitable, and may be preferred by some teachers, the building up of shared resources available to all in the English department is an essential component of good subject department planning and should be supported by school managements.

It is reported that continuing professional development (CPD) is being facilitated and encouraged in the majority of schools, although the evidence from discussion and documents suggests that participation in subject-specific CPD varied not only from school to school but also from teacher to teacher.

In most instances, school development planning has played a significant part in identifying and meeting wholeschool CPD needs, and staff development days have dealt with such issues as mixed-ability teaching and special needs. It should be borne in mind that good subject planning includes the identification of subject-specific CPD needs. Best practice was observed where teachers of English had strong links with local education centres and teachers' professional networks, subject associations, and the Second-Level Support Service. It is recommended that this good practice be adopted in all schools. Greater use of the internet by teachers of English to meet CPD needs is also encouraged.

Co-curricular activities are those that extend and reinforce the learning outcomes of the various syllabuses and programmes and that go beyond conventional classroom activities. In the case of English this covers an enormous range, and almost all schools provide co-curricular activities to varying degrees.

Theatre trips, debating, public speaking and writing competitions featured most prominently, while the production of the school play or of a magazine or yearbook was also widespread practice. Participation in the Writers in Schools scheme and links with local libraries, writers, arts groups, arts festivals and radio stations are less common, although some very good instances of collaboration with outside agencies have been reported. These are areas that could be further explored by many schools. This report commends the facilitation of such activities and the efforts made to ensure that they are purposeful and productive for the participating students.

Planning and Preparation for English

During the period surveyed the inspectors of English have noted an increasingly structured approach to subject planning. The most obvious manifestation of this was the significant increase in the number of planning documents available. Good planning for the teaching and learning of English requires a high level of collaboration among all the teachers of the subject, a schedule of meetings that facilitates both forward planning and review, and a focus on the aims and learning outcomes or skills appropriate to students and programmes.

Although in a few instances levels of co-operation and even communication between teachers were very low, and in many more instances the traditional view of the teacher as solo practitioner remained strong, co-operative work practices existed among the teachers of English in most schools. Discussions on such issues as the selection of texts and the placement of students took place as the need arose, and teachers are to be commended for the good levels of collegiality, involving practical and moral support, that were evident in many schools. However, informal co-operation is not a secure enough basis for building good planning practices that will be of enduring benefit to teachers and students.

The incidence of strong subject department structures is rising. The good English departments encountered during the inspections were marked by many or all of the following characteristics:

— a participative approach to planning for English

— the sharing of resources and of expertise, particularly in teaching strategies

— the facilitation and promotion of good practice by an active co-ordinator

— regular meetings, both formally scheduled and as issues arise, with agendas and records of decisions taken

— effective systems of communication within the department, with learning-support teachers, and with the management

— the distribution of routine tasks, such as setting papers and preparing resources to avoid the duplication of work

— an active approach to CPD.

Fewer than one in three of the schools inspected had all these features. Where a strong English department structure existed, the benefits were clear in the co-ordinated delivery of the subject throughout the school, the shared work load, and the good lines of communication with the school management and with related areas such as learning support. It is heartening, therefore, to note the greater movement towards the formation of English departments and the increasing recognition in schools of their role in lessening the burden of planning and preparation for the individual teacher and in strengthening the delivery of the subject.

In creating a strong and supportive subject department structure, the school's senior management and teachers of English should bear the following points in mind. The English department should have timetabled meetings at least three times in the academic year, with a formal agenda and minutes. The purpose of these meetings is to agree future plans and to review existing ones, both of which are continuous processes. The role and the responsibilities of the co-ordinator should be agreed as part of the English plan and should concentrate on organising and facilitating collaborative practices, including the sharing of information, tasks, resources, and expertise.

The increase in the volume of planning documents available has already been noted and is commended. Plans inspected ranged from the rudimentary to the comprehensive; most were at an early stage of development. The most basic consisted of content to be covered, usually through the naming of texts. Where other aspects of the syllabus were mentioned it was in very general terms, for example "Comprehension". More developed plans referred to texts and linked them with tasks. They also listed available resources, placed the work to be done within a clear time scale, and outlined methods of assessment, adding considerably to their usefulness. However, a weakness was often found in otherwise substantial plans in the area of planned learning outcomes. References to aims and objectives were frequently too general to be of much practical use. In other words, they lacked a focus on the specific skills to be acquired by students in each class or year group. It should be particularly noted, therefore, that best practice was observed where plans:

— were designed to achieve the aims and objectives of the relevant syllabus or programme

— referred specifically to skills and learning outcomes, linking them appropriately to texts

— suggested appropriate methods and constructive modes of assessment for these skills

— demonstrated an integrated approach to language and literature by making explicit links between the texts that students were reading and the development of students' writing.

A comprehensive plan should therefore show a progressive building of skills from first to sixth year. At a more basic level, it should prevent the unnecessary repetition of material and texts. Other useful components of comprehensive plans included a description of the co-ordinator's role, records of tasks allocated, the school's and the department's homework policy, relevant syllabus documents, the Department's circulars, and chief examiners' reports.

The practice of using the subject plan as a focus for department meetings was also noted and is commended. The amendments to the plan that may result from decisions taken at these meetings should be seen as an indication that the process of subject planning and the process of review and evaluation within a subject department are complementary. Every teacher of English should have either a printed copy of the plan or easy access to an electronic version of it. Where teachers engaged fully with the process of subject planning it had immediate practical benefits and played a valuable role in professional development. Of some concern, therefore, is the finding that the production of planning documents was occasionally seen as an end in itself, detached from the realities of teaching and learning. The view that the plan is a one-off task and can be consigned to a shelf once completed is neither an intended nor a desirable outcome of subject planning.

English departments should review their planning documents in the light of these observations. It is hoped that the significant minority of schools where subject plans for English have not yet been developed will find them a guide and an encouragement. In most schools, good individual planning was undertaken by many teachers. Best practice was seen where individual plans complemented the planning done by the department as a whole, for example where individual teachers planned a specific approach to a common text or topic to suit the particular classes they were teaching. Whether or not there was an agreed subject plan, individual plans consisted of more or less detailed schemes of work and were usually time-specific, often being written in diary fashion. Just as with the subject plan, the best individual schemes of work concentrated on objectives and learning outcomes and included assignments to be given to students that clearly related to these outcomes.

The preparation by individual teachers of resources to be used in lessons on particular writers, texts and topics was also widespread. These included documentary film clips, photographs shown on overhead or data projectors, photocopied articles, and, on occasion, actual objects. The practice of sharing the resources prepared by individual teachers among all members of the English teaching team on a reciprocal basis is to be encouraged.

Planning for English within the JCSP was good in the majority of schools offering the programme. It was clear that the relevant teachers in these schools were familiar with the range of JCSP support materials available and had incorporated them in their planning. Typically, the good planning observed was marked by

— a clear emphasis on the needs of this student cohort

— an appropriate use of target statements

— an imaginative and stimulating choice of material.

Where planning was poor there was little sense of the gradual building of skills and competence, and the range of material chosen was limited and unexciting. It is recommended that all those involved in the teaching of English within the JCSP familiarise themselves with the support materials and publications on the JCSP web site.

The good transition-year English programmes observed offered participants

— active and student-centred learning experiences, including cross-curricular work

— exposure to a range of texts from many genres

— experience of different modes of assessment, including assessment of oral presentations and project work

— opportunities to develop the skills and competence required in the senior cycle.

In relation to the last point above, where Leaving Certificate material is included in the transition-year programme it should be handled in a significantly different way and one that is appropriate to the objectives of the transition year, for example a performance of a play rather than an academic reading of it.

Transition-year English programmes were often not specific enough in relation to the development of writing skills. It is recommended that clear objectives for students' writing be stated in the programme plan, and that these be seen as a bridge between Junior Certificate and Leaving Certificate learning outcomes.

All transition-year students should have a copy of the programme, including the methods of assessment, thus giving them a measure of responsibility for their own progress. English departments in schools offering transition year would benefit from consulting the brief and helpful document Writing the Transition Year Programme. This will provide a useful checklist for schools that have a detailed written programme and will give the necessary framework to those that have not.

The LCA English and Communications programme combines prescribed activities and assignments with opportunities for teachers' and students' choice of texts and materials. Good programme planning in this area was characterised by

— a structure that emphasised the building of skills, thus increasing students' confidence and selfesteem

— a range of suitably challenging materials, including substantial creative texts in a variety of genres

— a choice of materials and methods designed to connect with and enrich the students' own experience.

Poor planning and a limited or unsuitable choice of material led to low student motivation. It is therefore strongly recommended that the LCA English and Communications programme be informed by the collective expertise of the English department and that the department build up specific resources both of materials and methods so as to deliver the programme successfully.

The choice of texts has a significant effect on the quality of the learning experience for students and on the level of their engagement with it. With specific reference to the junior cycle, the texts chosen in all genres were frequently from a very small and predictable pool. In a significant minority of schools, students read only one novel over the three years of the course, and had a very limited exposure to poetry. A further concern was the poor exposure to drama among ordinary-level students, with film completely replacing rather than complementing the study of a play.

Both the Junior Certificate syllabus and the teachers' guidelines emphasise the importance of students' experience of a diversity of texts. It is therefore strongly recommended that at least one appropriately challenging and stimulating novel be read in each junior-cycle year. In the choosing of first-year novels, best practice was observed where teachers liaised with feeder primary schools to avoid choosing novels already covered. The study of a play should be an integral part of the course; and students should encounter a range of poems appropriate to their developing skills and maturity over the course of the three years. The pool of texts should also be changed and added to regularly.

English textbooks of the anthology or compendium type were widely used. These should not be seen as forming the plan for English in the junior cycle, nor should they be the only resource available for the teaching of poetry and language skills in particular. The availability of audiotapes as an adjunct to the reading of novels and especially of plays was noted, and commended as good planning of resources, in a number of schools.

In general, the range and variety of texts chosen was greater at the Leaving Certificate level than in the junior cycle. English departments are to be commended where they have moved away from the more familiar texts and made choices on the basis of what is likely to work best for their students. Good practice was observed in schools where choice of text was managed so as to allow students to change level where necessary. This involved collaborative planning in the choice of accessible common texts and in some instances using the ordinary-level single text as a comparative text at the higher level. English departments should avoid choosing texts for the senior cycle that have already been studied in the junior cycle.

The choice of texts within the Leaving Certificate programme must be made in compliance with the relevant lists of prescribed material which are issued to schools annually and are on the department's web site. The chief examiners' reports for Leaving Certificate English at both levels in 2005 referred to a small number of instances where candidates had studied texts not on the course, with serious consequences for them in loss of marks.

In most schools, liaison between teachers of English and learning-support teachers was good. The practice of giving this liaison a structure through formal meeting times between the English department and learning-support teachers is to be commended and should be extended to improve the provision and delivery of literacy support.

Many of the schools where significant numbers of students have literacy difficulties were addressing this through the adoption of a wholeschool literacy policy, including information and training sessions for the whole staff from the learning-support co-ordinator and external learning-support trainers. The very good work being done by schools in this area has been warmly commended in many English inspection reports.

Where schools had embraced a wholeschool approach to literacy development there was very good support for less able students in building their vocabulary and language skills in a structured manner. In schools where such an approach has yet to be implemented, the progress of these students was less certain, and this is a cause for concern. The facilitation by school managements of staff development in the area of literacy support is to be commended, and this practice should be extended.

Teaching and Learning

A reliable indicator of a well-structured lesson is the communication to students of the purpose of the lesson at the outset. Where clear statements about the content of the lesson were made at the beginning, they were effective in establishing a sense of direction. Even better, but less common, was the practice of stating the purpose of the lesson in terms of learning activities and objectives. This approach was observed to engage and focus students' attention, thus assisting good classroom management.

Best practice was observed where these objectives were used in the summing up at the end of the lesson, reinforcing the sense of the lesson as a learning unit. This is the recommended practice. Where there was no explicit statement of lesson content a sense of purpose was established if the class was able to engage swiftly with the work planned for the lesson. Where no sense of purpose was evident, this reflected poor lesson planning.

The pacing of lessons was often well judged, with a good balance between the need to maintain interest and a sense of forward movement on the one hand and the need to ensure that enough time was given for new material to be understood on the other. Individual lesson content was generally well judged in relation to the time available.

Poor judgement of time occasionally led to inadequate recapitulation or to the hasty setting of homework at the end of the lesson. Less commonly, too little material or too few activities had been planned, resulting in dead time at the end of the lesson. Pacing often appeared too slow where a lesson lacked variety in content or in method of teaching; good planning is required to avoid the disengagement by students that this causes. Some very good practice was observed in junior-cycle classes where lessons were divided into two or three topic areas that were clearly linked either to previous work or to another topic in the same lesson. The good practice of linking lessons with prior learning was widespread.

Resources

Many of the resources commonly available in classrooms are so familiar as to be somewhat undervalued and therefore used less well than they could be. In particular, use of the board varied widely in quality. Best practice was observed where the well-organised use of the board served many functions:

— naming the topic or topics for the lesson

— recording in sequence the points arising out of whole-class discussion or group work

— listing key words or points as part of pre-reading or pre-writing activities

— working out problems in punctuation, spelling, and sentence structure

— displaying correct spelling and punctuation

— setting homework and other assignments.

Dividing the board so as to create a margin where spellings and new vocabulary were recorded separately is a commendable strategy that should be more widely used. Overhead projectors were used less widely but often to good effect, especially where a piece of text to be studied had been copied onto acetate and was then worked on or annotated during the lesson. A collection of such acetates is a useful addition to the English department's resources. It is imperative that all writing on the board or overhead projector be accurate and legible and that it serve students as a model for organising their own ideas before writing.

Visual texts, both film and still images, presented their own challenges. Although the still images chosen for class study were often multi-layered and subtle, the sometimes poor quality of the photocopies used made attention to detail very difficult. Images were not always subjected to a sufficiently rigorous analysis, nor was the opportunity to teach the specific vocabulary required always taken. A collection of still images colour-copied onto acetate or downloaded and shown on data projector would greatly assist visual analysis and the teaching and learning of terminology in this area.

The study of film was generally more focused, especially in the Leaving Certificate programme, although poor preparation in relation to the cueing and timing of film sequences shown in class was occasionally observed. In general, it should be recognised that the use of resources for teaching visual texts requires careful planning and preparation and that the perception that these texts are easy for students is false.

The most recent reports on performance in the Junior Certificate and Leaving Certificate examinations make instructive reading on this issue, and it is recommended that English departments study them carefully. Visually rich classrooms, with displays of posters and photographs, were seen to be a very useful resource, and this is an area for development in many schools.

The use of audiotapes and CDs was less widespread than it should be, given the wealth of resources available in these formats. Some very good practice was observed in relation to novels on tape, with students reading along silently, and it is recommended that this practice be used where appropriate, either to assist students' understanding or to draw their attention to key moments. Poetry and songs on tape were also used effectively.

Audio resources are especially applicable to drama; where used, they clearly added to students' engagement with and understanding of the play. Audiotapes are particularly recommended for the teaching of Shakespearean drama, where the complexities of the language may mean that students find the reading of parts too daunting. Audiotapes also provide an excellent resource for teasing out issues of characterisation and interpretation.

It is regrettable that in many classrooms the study of drama has become a study of the film of the play, which may differ substantially from the original text. On the other hand, listening to the play on audiotape focuses attention on words and tone, and provides space for the imagination in relation to action and gesture. While such textbooks were seen to provide stimulating and enjoyable material, two specific causes for concern also arose.

The first was the extent to which, following a lively reading and discussion of a text from the anthology, homework was assigned from the questions in the textbook, whether or not they truly reflected and captured the issues dealt with in the preceding discussion. A more selective use of textbook assignments is therefore recommended. The second concern arose where language skills, in particular grammar and syntax, were treated as a separate issue in textbooks. In practice this led to the teaching of language skills in isolation, whereas they should be grounded in the texts the students are reading.

The practice of taking English classes to the computer room was observed in a few schools but is much less widespread than is desirable. The process of drafting and editing which is essential to the development of students' writing skills can be carried out in an efficient and engaging way on wordprocessor. 5 Work on sentence structure, paragraphing and layout can be done particularly effectively, and the grammar, spelling and word-counting tools, carefully used, aid the development of proofreading skills.

Methods and Strategies

The inspectors of English observed the use of a wide range of teaching strategies. The effectiveness of these strategies varied, sometimes because of the nature of the student cohort and sometimes because of the level of preparation by the teacher. However, the most effective strategies were those that demanded the active participation of students, whether as engaged listeners, responsive readers, or purposeful writers.

The dominance of teacher talk, whether providing information and opinion or questioning students, was a strikingly consistent finding in inspections of English. As a teaching style this relies heavily on the ability of students to be an audience-literally a group of listeners. Where students could process the spoken word in an active and engaged way, and were confident enough to express their own sometimes dissenting views, this method worked well. However, even in these circumstances some variety in teaching methods is desirable. It must be said that too often the unvarying use of this teaching style led to passivity and disengagement on the part of students.

Where particularly good practice to secure students' participation was seen it was clear that there had been thorough planning and preparation and that the teacher exercised a firm yet friendly control. It was notable that pair and group work was successful where students had clear instructions before beginning the task and knew the purpose of their work, the time allotted, and the end result required. This was tested in a real sense when the pair or group had to report on their findings to the whole class, and this is recommended as an appropriate conclusion to such work. It is also recommended that students work in groups of no more than three, initially at least, and that the teacher control the formation of the groups.

Questioning was the most widely used of the teaching methods observed, but the purpose, context and style of questioning were often not considered carefully enough. In many instances questioning largely concentrated on testing the recall of facts or basic comprehension, leading at times to chorus answering unless questions were directed at named students.

Another common phenomenon observed was where the question sought a response to more complex issues, for example the mood or tone of a poem, but students were not given enough time to respond thoughtfully. Where this occurred, the work of expanding the response was actually done by the teacher, not the students. At its best, however, questioning was flexible and dynamic, in that it was appropriately applied to many different purposes and contributed greatly to lively and productive teaching and learning.

Questioning was used particularly effectively to help students see links between new material and prior learning and to push them towards more precise thinking and expression. It is recommended that the style and pace of questioning be varied according to its specific purpose and that students be made aware of the different types of questions. When used to check students' recall or grasp of facts, questioning should be directed at named students, not at the whole class. Higher-order questions, intended to encourage students to grapple with more complex material and to develop an informed personal opinion on it, should be open to a wide range of responses, and students must be given enough time to articulate such responses themselves.

While many teachers commented to the inspectors on the wide range of ability in most class groups, there was little evidence of differentiation in the teaching methods observed. The most common practice was that teachers organised class work so that more able students could work independently, leaving the teacher free to give assistance where required.

Rarely was the teacher's interaction with the class differentiated so as to ensure that all students had an opportunity to answer a question or to make a contribution at a level that was appropriate for them. However, some very good practice was observed where worksheets or other structured assignments began at a very manageable level and continued to more complex tasks, with useful prompts or writing frames to enable all students to develop their responses. It is recommended that English departments take an active approach to continuing professional development in the area of differentiation.

Skill Development

The emphasis on the acquisition and development of skills in the syllabuses and programmes dealt with in this report has been mentioned in the introduction. While good practice in this regard was observed in many schools, areas for improvement were also identified. The findings and recommendations given here relate to vocabulary-building and the development of expressive language, competence in the accurate and appropriate use of language, and the expansion of reading and writing skills across a range of genres.

Many teachers were adept at introducing sophisticated vocabulary to their students by using it in class discussion in such a way that the context or the use of a simpler synonym provided the necessary gloss.

Best practice was observed where students were then encouraged to make these words their own by using them in their own speaking and writing. Use of the board to reinforce the acquisition of new vocabulary is recommended, as is a greater use of dictionaries in the classroom. Very good practice was observed where teachers modelled the use of dictionaries by consulting them in class themselves and demonstrating their importance for vocabulary-building.

While the parallel translation of sophisticated vocabulary was seen to provide a useful bridge by which students could acquire a richer language themselves, this should not be confused with the undesirable practice of substituting paraphrase for the original text. This happened most often in the study of poetry, where attention to the patterns and resonances of the actual words on the page is really essential.

Another difficulty in the study of poetry occurred where the investigation of figurative language frequently concentrated too much on terms and definitions rather than on effect or purpose. It should be remembered that it is useful for students to master the terminology only insofar as it assists their understanding of and response to the poem. It is not an end in itself. It has already been noted that in many instances where lively class discussion was observed, students were encouraged to express their views and were assisted towards a more focused and articulate personal response through good and challenging questions posed by the teacher.

The expressive skills developed in such interchanges need to be carried through to writing tasks that will consolidate the work done orally. Where this happened, clear links between oral and written questions, and a consistent use of focused class discussion as a pre-writing exercise, resulted in good and substantial written work from students. This is commended as very good practice. Another good strategy for building their expressive skills was observed where students were given opportunities to make oral presentations to the class. This happened less frequently than is desirable and was seen most often in transition year and LCA. This good practice should be extended to all years and programmes.

An integrated approach to the teaching of language and literature is explicitly advocated in the Junior Certificate and Leaving Certificate English syllabuses. While this was implemented in a majority of schools, areas for development were also identified. In many instances, students were given writing tasks in specific genres which were based on characters and situations in a play or novel that they were studying. This is good practice. However, they should also be given good models of the specific genres of writing to guide them in creating the appropriate structure and register for their own compositions. It should be noted that the most recent chief examiners' reports for Junior Certificate and Leaving Certificate English recommend the use of exemplars to assist in the development of writing skills in various genres and styles.

Integrating the teaching of language and literature would also assist in developing the accuracy and maturity of students' spoken and written language and should be used much more widely than it is at present. In particular, aspects of sentence and paragraph structure are best learned from the study of exemplars drawn from the texts that students are reading, so that the emphasis is on the application of these skills for real-life purposes.

Where creative modelling or imitation was used to lead students towards more accomplished writing there was clear evidence of its effectiveness, and a more widespread use of this method is urged. In general, a more structured and incremental approach to the development of writing skills is necessary.

Accuracy in language and register will not be achieved without planning, drafting, rewriting, and editing. As these are actual stages in the real-life writing and publishing process, they should be directed towards a similar end in the school setting to encourage students to take the necessary pains to attain a worthy finished product.

In a number of schools, selected samples of students' finished work were published in the form of classroom displays, corridor or library display for an open day or parents' night, a space on the school web site, or a newsletter or magazine. This very good practice should be a feature in all schools. The use of ICT to teach editing skills was observed to be effective but not widespread, and its greater use for this purpose is recommended.

Wide reading in a variety of genres is a stated syllabus and programme aim, and the relevance of these points to the development of reading skills is clear. A minimalist approach to prescribed reading was a negative finding in a minority of English inspection reports.

In particular, the practice of reducing the comparative study for ordinary-level students to one written text and a film is an unnecessary and unacceptable minimising of the course. On the other hand, teachers were commended for the efforts made in many schools to offer all students a rich and varied experience of texts in a range of genres.

Pre-reading strategies served a useful purpose in arousing students' interest. These included inviting students to predict the story from the cover picture or blurb, and introducing concepts and vocabulary to attune students to the world of the text. The explicit teaching of such reading skills as skimming and scanning was also observed and commended.

Learning Evidence

In responses to questioning by the teacher and in interaction with the inspectors, students demonstrated a familiarity with the content of their courses in the majority of instances and generally revealed good recall of texts studied. However, they were not always aware of the need to support their views with reasoned argument. There were fewer competent responses to questions requiring a grasp of concepts, and a greater emphasis on higher-order questioning is recommended.

Students were for the most part willing to participate in class activity and in doing so demonstrated a positive attitude to learning. Instances of serious disengagement were uncommon. For the most part also students were organised and purposeful in their work, willing to address themselves to the task, and happy to ask for assistance or clarification. Where they were poorly prepared for class, for example not having the necessary books or copybooks with them, it appeared that they did not think that any sanctions would be applied. A firm wholeschool policy should be adopted to deal with this issue where it arises.

Good practice was observed where students' folders, copybooks and notes provided clear evidence of their progress. This also suggested a sense of shared responsibility for their own learning, which is a very desirable attitude to inculcate in students. Reviewing written work to eliminate errors in punctuation and spelling is a skill that must be explained and modelled by the teacher, but the aim of this process is to enable students to be their own proofreaders. Poor attitudes to written work and the maintenance of copybooks and folders were observed in a few instances, and these should not go unchecked. Specifically, students must know that certain minimal standards of presentation are required.

Students were generally learning at an appropriate pace and level. Where this was not the case they were being insufficiently challenged, and it should be pointed out that this was more likely to occur in classes perceived to be of lower ability. The level of students' work and engagement was higher where expectations of them were also appropriately high.

Classroom Management

The physical space was generally well managed so as to promote learning in an orderly and stimulating environment, and some very good examples of this were seen. Exceptions to this were seen where desks and chairs were either completely immovable or else appeared to be placed at random and where little effort had been made to make the room itself print-rich or visually interesting. Seating arrangements and classroom displays should maximise the potential for students' learning. The displaying of work should be done as a matter of course to celebrate and reward students' efforts.

The management of students was generally good, with many instances of a friendly yet respectful rapport between students and teachers. Seating plans and the movement of the teacher around the classroom were noted as practices contributing to good control and interaction.

The movement of the teacher around the room was seen to be particularly effective in promoting students' engagement and alertness, and in facilitating differentiated learning. It is therefore recommended. In almost all instances, interventions by the teacher both to deal with issues of behaviour and to assist specific students in difficulty were handled with commendable sensitivity and assurance.

The role of appropriate lesson content and pacing in maintaining students' involvement and co-operation was clearly observed, and there was particularly strong evidence of this in schools where a positive and active wholeschool approach had been taken to deal with challenging behaviour. This approach was praised in a number of English inspection reports, and its more widespread adoption is recommended. There were strongly positive findings on the level of encouragement given to students, and teachers are to be commended on the very high level of care and interest generally shown in their interaction with the students.

Enthusiasm among teachers of English for their subject and their work was encountered often, though not universally, and was communicated strongly to students in a variety of ways that reflected teachers' individual personalities. An obvious connection could be seen between the teacher's level of enthusiasm and the students' enjoyment of the subject. It is clearly good practice, therefore, for teachers of English to provide assistance and affirmation to each other, and for school managements to support them so that their enthusiasm is fostered and maintained.

ASSESSMENT AND ACHIEVEMENTS

While popular attention is overwhelmingly focused on terminal summative assessment, and in particular on the state examinations, assessment is of course a continuous activity and an integral part of students' learning. The most frequently used methods of assessment in the classroom were questioning of named students to test understanding and recall, . monitoring the progress of students doing writing or group assignments in class . oral and visual checking of homework . observation of students' level of engagement with class work.

The need for a greater use of more challenging questions has already been stated. While oral checking of homework is adequate and helpful for very short or factual tasks, it is recommended that thorough checking of substantial assignments be done outside the classroom. It is important that the setting and testing of spellings be done in a systematic way which will assist poor spellers to see helpful patterns. That being said, the emphasis on accurate spelling is to be encouraged.

Assessment for learning is the process of using assessment not to test what students have learned but to decide where the learners are in their learning, where they need to go, and how best to get there. A positive observation in inspections of English was that assessment for learning is becoming more widespread and better understood. It is recommended that schools consult the relevant material published by the National Council for Curriculum and Assessment and available on their web site.

Homework

Considerable variations in practice regarding homework were observed. These variations related to the frequency with which work was set and marked, the thoroughness of marking, the adequacy and promptness of feedback to students, and the care with which homework was done and kept. Homework was set regularly in the majority of instances.

The marking of homework ranged from a bare tick on the page to specific and detailed comment and correction. Clearly the latter approach has the combined virtues of assisting students' progress and validating the efforts they are making. Substantial homework should therefore be marked with helpful and appropriately critical comment.

Once students have been taught the basic rules of punctuation and the correction of common errors they should be required to revise and correct their work carefully before submitting it, a practice that is best begun in first year. Students in third year and in the senior cycle should be expected to read over their work with particular care in order to eliminate any errors they commonly make.

Homework will be of a higher quality if it follows through from class work, and care should be taken to set homework that reflects class activity and discussion and consolidates learning. Of particular concern is the fact that the extended composition is not featuring as it should in homework. Some very good practice was observed where students carefully maintained folders containing their work, enabling them to develop a sense of their progress and assisting them with revision.

Assess Incoming Students

Both standardised diagnostic tests and entrance tests devised by the school were used frequently to assess incoming students. In relation to the former, most tests used in schools are not norm-referenced to the Irish school population. Therefore, it is recommended that caution be exercised when using data constructed from them on reading ages and general ability levels, especially for the purpose of placing students or withdrawing them from mainstream classes.

Students identified by these as requiring remediation should be monitored and re-tested regularly by the learning-support teacher. In addition, diagnostic tests should be administered appropriately by trained personnel for the purpose of assisting students' progress. Where schools devised their own entrance tests, usually in English, Irish, and mathematics, those responsible for the English test are advised to familiarise themselves with the primary curriculum for English to assist them in designing appropriate assessments.

School Examinations

The absence of common assessment is particularly unacceptable where decisions on students' placement in second or third year are made on the basis of examination performance at the end of first or second year. Where this practice obtained, English inspection reports strongly recommended that it be replaced with common assessment. Where students are set in fifth year it is recommended that their placement be confirmed by a common assessment early in the year. This has the added bonus of assisting students who have an unrealistic sense of the level of work required for higher-level English to make an informed and timely decision about the level best suited to them.

The appropriate preparation of common papers, together with the necessary agreed marking schemes, should be included in subject planning. It should be noted that such a system permits flexibility in the choice of texts, because open or alternative questions can be set in these areas.

An important aspect of preparation for examinations, and indeed of assessment for learning, is the sharing of assessment criteria with students. Again this practice was found in a minority of schools. At the simplest level, first-year students should know in advance what marks will be awarded in different sections of the paper and what approaches to answering will be best rewarded, and this practice should be followed and developed in subsequent years.

In the senior cycle, students should be conversant with the criteria of assessment used in the marking of Leaving Certificate English. Introducing these only at the stage of mock examinations militates against their usefulness to students. In this regard, teachers are reminded of the very useful document Assessment Advice to Students, issued by the Inspectorate at the time of the introduction of the present Leaving Certificate English syllabus and available on the web site of the Teaching English Support Service (TESS).

In a number of schools where students were to take state examinations on tape or by voice-activated computer their examination preparation included practice with these media. This requires the co-operation of all subject teachers and provides a very good indication of wholeschool support for students with special needs.

Monitoring Achievements

While it is the responsibility of the school management to maintain records of school examination results, it was expected that teachers would keep their own records of students' achievement in homework and other assignments, as well as school examinations. This was not always found to be the case. It is recommended that teachers of English maintain their own records in order to monitor students' progress and achievement effectively and thus be able to take remedial action where necessary.

These records can be used to inform decisions on students' placement or on referral for learning support. Where good systems of tracking students' achievement existed they were also used appropriately to identify underperformance by able students and provided good evidence in discussions with the students themselves and with their parents.

Most schools carry out some analysis of students' performance in the state examinations in order to compare the results achieved with those expected, and to measure the students' achievements against national figures while taking account of school context factors. It was most commendable that a number of schools with a high intake of students with literacy difficulties were developing policies to encourage the raising of students' expectations and a consequent improvement in their attainment.

The important role played by raising students' expectations was clear in these cases, but preceding this was a belief by the management and staff that students could indeed achieve more. Where such a belief in students' potential did not exist, a depressive effect on students' expectations and consequently on their achievement was observed. It is recommended, therefore, that English departments take an active approach to underachievement, especially where this leads students to choose a lower level than their abilities warrant.

5

Teaching English as a Foreign Language

TEFL or (Teaching English as a Foreign Language) programs, like TESL courses, refer to professional courses wherein non-English speaking people are trained in the English language. The only difference in this case is that the teaching programs are conducted in non-English speaking regions. Training programs for TEFL are usually conducted in English-speaking regions (although this is not a rule) but the coaching is offered in the student's native land.

With the growing importance of English (both written and conversational), TEFL is becoming a rewarding career option day-by-day. People trained as EFL teachers are usually appointed by commercial language schools, government departments, large companies and other renowned private and voluntary organizations like The British Council. They are also offered lucrative jobs and fixed-term contracts abroad.

TEFL instructors help their students improve their English writing and speaking ability by packing their instructions with the most useful information, presenting it in an extremely interesting manner. They impart their knowledge through various TEFL lessons to develop the four basic language skills of listening, speaking, reading and writing of the learners. Consequently, the job involves a lot of researching and planning on the part of the teacher.

As an instructor, you can make use of varied course materials and a variety of audio-visual aids to assist your students. You will also need to boost their confidence by engaging them in social and cultural activities or by taking them on outings. You can also try teaching on 'one-to-one' basis. Whatever be your approach, you ought to make the learning process easy and enjoyable to ensure success.

There is no recognized/certified organization to oversee the issuance of qualifications in general and hence there is no accepted standard qualification. The qualification of an instructor is usually decided by the organization for which the coach is to be recruited. Thus, in the European nations, an undergraduate degree and a TEFL/TESL certification is the average requirement. In USA, the basic qualification is a Master's degree in TESOL. In some nations, far less qualified instructors are appointed. Institutions like Berlitz do not recognize the CELTA / CertTESOL and train their teachers as per their own standards.

However, much we say that there are no set standards/ qualifications for being appointed as a TEFL coach or instructor, most commercial professional ventures are quite discriminating in their choice. TEFL certification courses and core curriculums help you develop all the positive skills and techniques that you need to become a successful EFL instructor.

Thus, you are tutored in the ways of training your students in grammar and vocabulary. Classroom management, motivating students and advanced trainings that help your students attain mastery over spoken and written English are some other tricks being imparted through these programs. In brief, the TEFL certification is a proof of your efficiency as an EFL instructor and most employers judge you on its basis.

Certification courses like CELTA, CELTYL, CertTESOL, etc. are conducted at a number of campuses in both UK and USA. Localized certification courses are also offered by individual organizations or institutions. You can even opt for a certification course online.

As a career, TEFL promises a good pay packet in addition to creating opportunities for you to visit interesting destinations. Overseas teaching ventures as a TEFL instructor help you with your career prospects. Exposure to different cultures and traditions, likewise, help you make all-round progress as an individual.

Best Methods of Foreign Language Instruction

It is now well established that young children tend to absorb relatively easily any language that they are surrounded by, and they appear to learn to speak a new language more easily than adults do.Compared to an older student, a child's language learning advantage is greatest in the area of pronunciation, somewhat weaker in the area of grammar usage, and slight when considering the size of their vocabulary. Still, the apparent overall benefit of early learning is leading many to implement foreign language programs in elementary school or even earlier.

Is this the best or even an advisable use of resources, especially children's time? The answer depends on what you want to achieve and how much you are willing to invest. A few hours a week of foreign language instruction focusing on learning words, songs, and a few ritualized exchanges is good for cultural exposure and appreciation, but do not expect real mastery. The implication of the research is not so much that one should start language teaching early - say, age 6 and expect spectacular results, but rather that the teaching should be age appropriate. When considering the "earlier is better" approach, three points often are overlooked:

— A young child tends to absorb a language through massive amounts of input and exposure, while explicit learning, involving rules and systematic practice, plays an important role for adolescents and adults.

— The impact of age of learning on ultimate proficiency is not always clear cut; in other words, some child learners end up with accents and incomplete second language grammars, and some adult learners become, for all practical purposes, as skilled as native speakers.

— While young learners are more likely than older students to ultimately speak a new language like native speakers, adolescents and adults actually learn foreign languages faster.

If proficiency is the goal, teaching young children a foreign language in an age-appropriate manner means providing a full-immersion education,taught by teachers who know the language well. Such programs simulate the environment of growing up with a language by:

— Integrating the second language with instruction in other subjects;

— Giving learners ample opportunities to engage in meaningful discourse with other students and teachers using the foreign language;

— Exposing learners to a variety of native speakers of the target language; and

— Focusing instruction on attaining the language skills needed for communicating about and understanding academic subject matter, not on mastering a foreign language for its own sake.

Some parents and teachers may be concerned that total immersion in a foreign language could impede a child's grasp of English and ability to learn other subjects. However, studies have shown that, while there can be an initial lag in English achievement, fullimmersion students catch up, scoring at least as well as other students on verbal and mathematics skills.They may even exceed monolingual children on some measures of cognitive processing.

Teaching Older Students

Immersion is not the only efficient way to learn a language. For older students, effective foreign language instruction includes direct teaching, systematic practice involving rules and grammar, and plenty of opportunities for conversation. It should be aimed at having students express and understand fully formed ideas and phrases, as well as learn the language's structure. A balanced instructional approach is vital. Too much focus on meaning fails to create the knowledge of structure necessary for anything beyond the most basic conversational skills. At the same time, while teaching structures directly is highly productive,an over-reliance on structure, perhaps through endless mechanical drills, can lead to the "boredom factor" -students want to actually communicate in a foreign language, not labor over the nuts and bolts.

In the proper dosage, focusing on the foundations of grammar and language structures will support a student's ability to express himself or herself readily. There are many ways to draw attention to the form of a language, depending on the student's aptitude, motivation, and previous experience and on the educational and learning goals of the student and the teaching program. Much research is available to guide educators in managing the balance between structure and meaning.

As with any type of learning, students' individual differences have an impact on how well each one grasps a subject. For adolescents and adults, a student's aptitude and motivation can be key factors in his or her foreign language learning. Aptitude for language learning can be measured through specialized tests,and large amounts of research suggest that it is the second most important language learning characteristic after age.Foreign language aptitude consists of several components including sensitivity to sound, which is important for pronunciation; sensitivity to structure, which affects a student's grasp of grammar; and memory, which can determine how well a student learns and retains vocabulary.

Furthermore, the precise impact of a student's foreign language aptitude is affected by three important variables - age; type of exposure to the language; and "linguistic distance," or the degree of difference between the native and the foreign language. In the end, aptitude, while difficult to define, clearly is an important factor for adolescents and adults learning a foreign language in the classroom.In conjunction with aptitude, foreign language mastery also is enhanced when a student is sufficiently motivated to learn a language, for example, to gain employment, travel, or integrate into a community.

Learning and Teaching Styles

In Foreign and Second Language Education Students learn in many ways-by seeing and hearing; reflecting and acting; reasoning logically and intuitively; memorizing and visualizing. Teaching methods also vary. Some instructors lecture, others demonstrate or discuss; some focus on rules and others on examples; some emphasize memory and others understanding. How much a given student learns in a class is governed in part by that student's native ability and prior preparation but also by the compatibility of his or her characteristic approach to learning and the instructor's characteristic approach to teaching.

The ways in which an individual characteristically acquires, retains, and retrieves information are collectively termed the individual's learning style. Learning styles have been extensively discussed in the educational psychology literature and specifically in the context of language learning by Oxford and her colleagues, and over 30 learning style assessment instruments have been developed in the past three decades.

Serious mismatches may occur between the learning styles of students in a class and the teaching style of the instructor, with unfortunate potential consequences. The students tend to be bored and inattentive in class, do poorly on tests, get discouraged about the course, and may conclude that they are no good at the subject of the course and give up. Instructors, confronted by low test grades, unresponsive or hostile classes, poor attendance, and dropouts, may become overly critical of their students (making things even worse) or begin to question their own competence as teachers. In this chapter, we will explore the following questions:

1. Which aspects of learning style are particularly significant in foreign and second language education?
2. Which learning styles are favored by the teaching styles of most language instructors?
3. What can be done to address the educational needs of all students in foreign and second language classes?

Dimensions of Learning Style

In the sections that follow, we describe five dichotomous learning style dimensions derived from work of Felder et al., indicating the ways in which the educational needs of students with strong preferences for certain poles of the dimensions are not met by traditional approaches to language instruction. The concluding section offers a summary of suggestions for meeting the needs of those students.

The proposed learning style dimensions may be defined in terms of the answers to the following five questions:

1. What type of information does the student preferentially perceive: sensory-sights, sounds, physical sensations, or intuitive-memories, ideas, insights?
2. Through which modality is sensory information most effectively perceived: visual-pictures, diagrams, graphs, demonstrations, or verbal-written and spoken words and formulas?
3. How does the student prefer to process information: actively-through engagement in physical activity or discussion, or reflectively-through introspection?
4. How does the student progress toward understanding: sequentially-in a logical progression of small incremental steps, or globally-in large jumps, holistically?
5. With which organization of information is the student most comfortable: inductive- facts and observations are given, underlying principles are inferred, or deductive-principles are given, consequences and applications are deduced?

Sensing and Intuitive Learners

In his theory of psychological types, Jung introduced sensation and intuition as the two ways in which people tend to perceive the world. Sensing involves observing, gathering data through the senses; intuition involves indirect perception by way of the subconscious accessing memory, speculating, imagining. Everyone uses both faculties constantly, but most people tend to favor one over the other. The strength of this preference has been assessed for millions of people using the Myers-Briggs Type Indicator (MBTI), and the different ways in which sensors and intuitors approach learning have been characterized.

Sensors tend to be concrete and methodical, intuitors to be abstract and imaginative. Sensors like facts, data, and experimentation; intuitors deal better with principles, concepts, and theories. Sensors are patient with detail but do not like complications; intuitors are bored by detail and welcome complications. Sensors are more inclined than intuitors to rely on memorization as a learning strategy and are more comfortable learning and following rules and standard procedures. Intuitors like variety, dislike repetition, and tend to be better equipped than sensors to accommodate new concepts and exceptions to rules. Sensors are careful but may be slow; intuitors are quick but may be careless.

Ehrman and Oxford studied learning strategies and teaching approaches preferred by sensors and intuitors in an intensive language training program. The sensors used a variety of memorization strategies like internal drills and flash cards, liked class material that might better be described as practical than fanciful, and liked highly structured and well organized classes with clear goals and milestones for achievement. Intuitors preferred teaching approaches that involved greater complexity and variety, tended to be bored with drills, and were better able than sensors to learn independently of the instructor's teaching style.

Basic language instruction that involves a great deal of repetitive drill and memorization of vocabulary and grammar is better suited to sensors than intuitors. If there is too much of this sort of thing without a break, the intuitors who constitute the majority of the class, if Moody's results are representative-may become bored with the subject and their course performance may consequently deteriorate. On the other hand, strongly intuitive language instructors may tend to move too quickly through the basic vocabulary and rules of grammar in their eagerness to get to "the more interesting material"-grammatical complexities, nuances of translation, linguistic concepts, and cultural considerations. While the intuitive students may enjoy these topics, overemphasizing such material may result in insufficient grounding in the building blocks of the language. The sensors, in particular, may then start to fall behind and do poorly on homework and tests.

Effective instruction reaches out to all students, not just those with one particular learning style. Students taught entirely with methods antithetical to their learning style may be made too uncomfortable to learn effectively, but they should have at least some exposure to those methods to develop a full range of learning skills and strategies. To be effective, language instruction should therefore contain elements that appeal to sensors and other elements that appeal to intuitors. The material presented in every class should be a blend of concrete information (word definitions, grammatical rules) and concepts (syntactical and semantic information, linguistic and cultural background information), with the percentage of each being chosen to fit the level of the course (beginning, intermediate, or advanced) and the age and level of sophistication of the students.

Visual and Verbal Learners

We propose to classify the ways people receive sensory information as visual, verbal, and other (tactile, gustatory, olfactory). Visual learners prefer that information be presented visually-in pictures, diagrams, flow charts, time lines, films, and demonstrations-rather than in spoken or written words. Verbal learners prefer spoken or written explanations to visual presentations. The third category (touch, taste, smell) plays at most a marginal role in language instruction and will not be addressed further.

This categorization is somewhat unconventional in the context of the learning style literature, in which sensory modalities are classified as visual, auditory, and kinesthetic. Since the five human senses are seeing, hearing, touching, tasting, and smelling, we suggest that "kinesthetic" does not properly belong on a list of sensory input modalities. A student's preference for motion or physical activity of some sort during the learning process belongs in a separate learning style category: our proposed system and Kolb's model place it in the active/reflective dimension, and the familiar model based on Jung's typology includes it in the extravert-introvert dimension.

The distinction between the visual-auditory and visual-verbal classifications has to do with whether reading prose is more closely related to seeing pictures (which leads to the visualauditory contrast) or to hearing speech (visualverbal). Three mechanisms have been proposed for the process of extracting lexical significance from written words): direct access (the reader jumps directly from the printed form of the word to its lexical meaning), indirect access (the printed words are translated internally into sounds before information about their meaning can be located in lexical memory), and dual encoding (lexical memory can be reached either directly or indirectly). An extensive body of research supports a form of the dual encoding hypothesis.

Direct access is possible when words are familiar or when artificial conditions imposed in a research setting make speech encoding inefficient; however, when material is unfamiliar or difficult, lexical memory is speech accessed. The implication is that expository prose of the sort one finds in books and on classroom chalkboards is much more likely to be speech-mediated than directly accessed when silently read, and so belongs in the verbal rather than the visual category.

Most people extract and retain more information from visual presentations than from written or spoken prose, while most language instruction is verbal, involving predominantly lectures, writing in texts and on chalkboards, and audiotapes in language laboratories. Given the preference of most students for visual input, one would expect the last of these modes of presentation in particular to be unpopular. When community college students were asked to rank-order 13 instructional modes, including lectures, discussion, slides, field trips, and audiotapes, audiotapes ranked at or near the bottom for the overwhelming majority of students surveyed.

Recent studies of learning styles in foreign language education consistently place reading in the visual category, implying that instructors can meet the needs of visual learners solely by relying on written instructional material. Certainly visual learners learn better if they see and hear words in the target language, but so do auditory learners: presenting the same material in different ways invariably has a reinforcing effect on retention. The challenge to language instructors is to devise ways of augmenting their verbal classroom presentation with nonverbal visual material-for example, showing photographs, drawings, sketches, and cartoons to reinforce presentation of vocabulary words, and using films, videotapes, and dramatizations to illustrate lessons in dialogue and pronunciation.

Active and Reflective Learners

The complex mental processes by which perceived information is converted into knowledge can be conveniently grouped into two categories: active experimentation and reflective observation. Active processing involves doing something in the external world with the information-discussing it or explaining it or testing it in some way-and reflective processing involves examining and manipulating the information introspectively. An active learner is someone with more of a natural tendency toward active experimentation than toward reflective observation, and conversely for a reflective learner.

Active learners learn well in situations that enable them to do something physical and reflective learners learn well in situations that provide them with opportunities to think about the information being presented. The more opportunities students have to both participate and reflect in class, the better they will learn new material and the longer they are likely to retain it.

Language classes in which all students are relegated to passive roles, listening to and observing the instructor and taking notes, do little to promote learning for either active or reflective learners. Language classes should therefore include a variety of active learning experiences, such as conversations, enactment of dialogues and minidramas, and team competitions, and reflective experiences, such as brief writing exercises and question formulation exercises.

Small-group exercises can be extremely effective for both active and reflective learners. Pose a question or problem and have students come up with answers working in groups of three, with one group member acting as recorder. Such exercises engage all the students, not just the small minority who typically participate in class, and are a rich source of responses and material for subsequent discussion. The exercises also relieve the monotony of continuous lectures. In our experience, as little as five minutes of group work in a 50-minute period can be enough to maintain the students' attention for the entire class.

Group work must be used with care, however: simply telling students to work together on problems or projects can do more harm than good. Most references on cooperative learning point out that students often respond negatively to group work at first, and that the benefits of the approach are fully realized when the group work is structured to assure such features as positive interdependence, individual accountability, and appropriate uses of teamwork and interpersonal skills. Reid studied students from a variety of ethnic backgrounds and found that every background expressed a minor or negative preference for group work, with English speakers giving it the lowest rating. When language students have been taught cooperative skills, however, they showed positive results in both language skill and altruism.

Sequential and Global Learners

Sequential learners absorb information and acquire understanding of material in small connected chunks, and global learners take in information in seemingly unconnected fragments and achieve understanding in large holistic leaps. Before global learners can master the details of a subject they need to understand how the material being presented relates to their prior knowledge and experience, a perspective that relatively few instructors routinely provide. Consequently, strongly global learners may appear slow and do poorly on homework and tests until they grasp the total picture, but once they have it they can often see connections that escape sequential learners. On the other hand, sequential learners can function with incomplete understanding of course material, but they may lack a grasp of the broad context of a body of knowledge and its interrelationships with other subjects and disciplines.

Many authors who have done research on cognitive or learning styles have noted the importance of this dichotomous pairing, and various terms have been used to describe categories that appear to have points in common with what we term the sequential and global categories: analytic and global; field-independent and field-dependent; serialistic and holistic; left-brained and right-brained; atomistic and holistic; sequential and random. Luria's working brain model postulates successive and simultaneous modes of processing, and Pask similarly distinguishes between stringing and clumping modes of coding information and structuring responses.

Oxford proposes that this learning style dimension can be tapped through studies of brain hemisphericity. She cites studies of Leaver suggesting that left-brain (sequential) thinkers deal more easily with grammatical structure and contrastive analysis, while right-brain (global) thinkers are better at learning language intonation and rhythms. Sequential learners gravitate toward strategies that involve dissecting words and sentences into component parts and are comfortable with structured teaching approaches that stress grammatical analysis;

global learners prefer holistic strategies such as guessing at words and searching for main ideas, and may respond well to relatively unstructured approaches like community language learning that might not appeal to sequential learners.

Inductive and Deductive Learners

Induction is a reasoning progression that proceeds from particulars (observations, measurements, data) to generalities (rules, laws, theories). Deduction proceeds in the opposite direction. In inductive presentation of classroom material, one makes observations and infers governing or correlating principles; in deductive presentation one starts with axioms, principles, or rules, deduces consequences, and formulates applications. As with the previous dimensions, students may have moderate or strong preferences for one or the other presentation mode; in particular, they may prefer deductive presentation because of its relatively high level of structure.

A large percentage of classroom teaching in every subject is primarily or exclusively deductive, probably because deduction is an efficient and elegant way to organize and present material that is already understood. However, there is considerable evidence that incorporating a substantial inductive component into teaching promotes effective learning. Inductive reasoning is thought to be an important component in academic achievement.

Current cognitive research emphasizes the importance of prior knowledge in learning; introducing new material by linking it to observed or previously known material is essentially inductive. The benefits claimed for inductive instructional approaches include increased academic achievement and enhanced abstract reasoning skills, longer retention of information, and improved ability to apply principles.

Insofar as foreign languages are concerned, we propose that the distinction between induction and deduction is akin to the distinction between language acquisition and learning. To acquire a language means to pick it up gradually, gaining the ability to communicate with it without necessarily being able to articulate the rules. Individuals absorb what they can from the abundant and continuous input that bombards them; they cannot grasp all they hear, but each day increases their ability to understand, retain, and use in conversation what they have taken in.

Throughout the process they gain in their ability to transfer strategies, make assumptions about the new language system, formulate and test rules, and either keep or abandon them. They continue this process until they fossilize, which they may do as soon as they feel they have learned what they need to in order to communicate in the language. In its progression from specifics to generalizations, acquisition is an inductive process.

On the other hand, language learning is a largely conscious process that involves formal exposure to rules of syntax and semantics followed by specific applications of the rules, with corrective feedback reinforcing correct usage and discouraging incorrect usage. The flow of the learning process from general to specific suggests its characterization as a deductive process.

Three well-known approaches illustrate deductive and inductive approaches to language instruction. The first is the grammartranslation method, rooted in the formal teaching of Latin and Greek that prevailed in Europe for many centuries. This method involves the translation of literary texts followed by explanation of rules of grammar.

Grammar-translation is the most deductive approach. A later approach is the direct method, in which classes are taught entirely in the target language; grammar is taught inferentially and plays a secondary role to oral communication. This approach, which was in vogue in many countries throughout the nineteenth century, is almost purely inductive.

The third approach is the audio-oral method, according to which language is a set of habits with vocabulary being of secondary concern. In this method, which was influenced by behavioral psychology and structural linguistics, students learn by repeating structural patterns and eventually automatize the structures, aided by positive reinforcement provided by the teacher. This approach combines acquired verbal skills (inductive) with learned reading and writing skills (deductive), with emphasis on the former. Advocates of the oral method have assumed that language learning is an inductive rather than a deductive process. Many common instructional techniques essentially fall into this category, although all may involve some deductive elements.

A long-standing controversy in language education has to do with whether languages can be acquired in the classroom or only learned. Brown, McLaughlin, and Gregg believe that both learning and acquisition may go on in classrooms. Krashen and Terrell hold that acquisition can only occur in natural settings, but later admit that "despite our conclusion that language teaching is directed at learning and not acquisition, we think that it is possible to encourage acquisition very effectively in the classroom". We agree, and believe that the key question facing language educators is, what classroom conditions and procedures facilitate the occurrence of language acquisition?

An important consideration in attacking this question has to do with the use to which an acquired or learned language is likely to be applied. By its very nature, language acquisition is more likely to manifest in oral fluency than in correct utilization of the written language and conversely for language learning.

Complete command of a language thus involves both acquisition-an inductive process, required to speak fluently-and learning-a deductive process, required to write grammatically. The two processes are not competitive but complementary, just as inductive and deductive reasoning are essential and coequal components of the scientific method. By analogy, it would appear that an ideal classroom setting for teaching a foreign language would be one that stimulates and facilitates both inductive and deductive learning processes, both acquisition and learning.

Validity and Utility of Proposed Learning Style

Several critical points can legitimately be raised regarding the proposed learning style categories. The categories are by no means comprehensive: no finite number of dimensions could ever encompass the totality of individual student differences, and components of other learning style models in the references cited in the introductory section also play important roles in determining how students receive and process information. Moreover, the dimensions have not been shown to be fully independent, and validated instruments to assess individual preferences on all of them do not exist.

The teaching style with which students feel most comfortable may not correspond to the style that enables them to learn most effectively. Having said all that, we would add that these disclaimers do not limit the usefulness of this or any other model. Although it can be helpful for an instructor to know the distribution of learning styles in a class, the point is not to place all students into one or another style category and to teach each student exclusively according to his or her preferred style.

Our hypothesis is that language instructors who adapt their instruction to address both poles of each of the five given dimensions should come close to providing an optimal learning environment for most students in a class.

Multistyle Approach to Foreign Language Education

Studies show that matching teaching styles to learning styles can significantly enhance academic achievement, student attitudes, and student behavior at the primary and secondary school level, at the college level, and specifically in foreign language instruction. This is not to say that the best thing one can do for one's students is to use their preferred modes of instruction exclusively. Students will inevitably be called upon to deal with problems and challenges that require the use of their less preferred modes, and so should regularly be given practice in the use of those modes. However, Smith and Renzulli caution that stress, frustration, and burnout may occur when students are subjected over extended periods of time to teaching styles inconsistent with their learning style preferences.

A point no educational psychologist would dispute is that students learn more when information is presented in a variety of modes than when only a single mode is used. The point is supported by a research study carried out several decades ago, which concluded that students retain 10 percent of what they read, 26 percent of what they hear, 30 percent of what they see, 50 percent of what they see and hear, 70 percent of what they say, and 90 percent of what they say as they do something. What must be done to achieve effective foreign language learning is to balance instructional methods, somehow structuring the class so that all learning styles are simultaneously-or at least sequentially-accommodated.

The prospect of tailoring language instruction to somehow accommodate 32 (25) different learning styles might seem forbidding to instructors. This reaction is understandable. Teaching styles are made up of the methods and approaches with which instructors feel most comfortable; if they tried to change to completely different approaches they would be forced to work entirely with unfamiliar, awkward, and uncomfortable methods, probably with disastrous results from the students' point of view. Fortunately, instructors who wish to address a wide variety of learning styles need not make drastic changes in their instructional approach. The way they normally teach addresses the needs of at least five of the specified learning style categories: regular use of at least some of the instructional techniques given below should suffice to cover the remaining five.

— *Motivate learning.* As much as possible, teach new material (vocabulary, rules of grammar) in the context of situations to which the students can relate in terms of their personal and career experiences, past and anticipated, rather than simply as more material to memorize (intuitive, global, inductive).

— *Balance concrete information* (word definitions, rules for verb conjugation and adjective-noun agreement) (sensing) and conceptual information (syntactical and semantic patterns, comparisons and contrasts with the students' native language) (intuition) in every course at every level. The balance does not have to be equal, and in elementary courses it may be shifted heavily toward the sensing side, but there should periodically be something to capture the intuitors' interest.

— *Balance structured teaching approaches that emphasize formal training* (deductive, sequential) with more open-ended unstructured activities that emphasis conversation and cultural contexts of the target language (inductive, global).

— *Make liberal use of visuals.* Use photographs, drawings, sketches, and cartoons to illustrate and reinforce the meanings of vocabulary words. Show films, videotapes, and live dramatizations to illustrate lessons in texts (visual, global.)

— Assign some repetitive drill exercises to provide practice in basic vocabulary and grammar (sensing) but don't overdo it (intuitive).

— Do not fill every minute of class time lecturing and writing on the board. Provide intervals-however brief-for students to think about what they have been told; assign brief writing exercises (reflective). Raise questions and problems to be worked on by students in small groups; enact dialogues and mini-dramas; hold team competitions (active).

— Give students the option of cooperating on at least some homework assignments (active).

— Active learners generally learn best when they interact with others; if they are denied the opportunity to do so they are being deprived of their most effective learning tool.

— Balance inductive and deductive presentation of course material. Instruct some or all of the class in the language being taught, to facilitate language acquisition and develop skill in oral communication (inductive). In parallel, provide explicit instruction in syntax and semantics to facilitate formal language learning and develop skill in written communication and interpretation (deductive).

Instructors confronted with this list might feel that it is impossible to do all that in a course and still cover the syllabus. Their concern is not unreasonable: extensive use of some of the recommended approaches-particularly those involving opportunities for student activity during class-could indeed add to the time it takes to present a given body of material. The idea, however, is not to adopt all the techniques at once but rather to pick several that look feasible and try them on an occasional basis; keep the ones that work; drop the others; and try one or two more later in the course or in the next course. In this way a teaching style that is both effective for students and comfortable for the instructor will evolve naturally, with a potentially dramatic effect on the quality of learning that subsequently occurs.

Curriculum Organization

In designing foreign language (FL) curricula an important but often overlooked concern is effective organization. Many FL programs give careful thought to linguistic content and sequencing, and instructional materials and activities, but they neglect those factors that relate to the structure and processes for implementing the curriculum. Matters as basic as physical space, classroom temperature, number of students, or time of day can also make a major difference in the way a teacher conducts a class and in the way the learners receive instruction. These are some of the concerns relating to the organizational dimension in FL curriculum planning.

Bellon and Handler identify three areas of curriculum organization:

— resources: time; people; instructional materials; facilities, and equipment.

— organizational process: the interactional network of the resources serving the curriculum.

— program units within the organization: all the other extra-curricular programs within the institution to support the goals of the curriculum.

The "fit" of these three organizational concerns with the goals and objectives of the curriculum is crucial to its successful implementation.

Resources

A curriculum cannot operate without resources. The amount and kind of resources available are important, but especially important is the way they are allocated and used. Take time, for example. An intensive FL curriculum may allocate more time for beginning learners and less time for advanced learners. A daily schedule might have beginning learners in class for six hours while the intermediate learners may attend for four hours and the advanced for only two. If the class schedule has been set based on curriculum goals, time will be allocated effectively. But if the decisions for scheduling have been based on the availability of teachers or classroom space or on some other factor unrelated to the goals and objectives of the curriculum, then the schedule may not be supportive of learning.

In many FL programs, the assignment of teachers to classes is one of the most challenging considerations in resource allocation. Many teachers who have been with a program for several years expect the privileges of seniority. These privileges can lead to their teaching the more desirable classes while new teachers are given the left-over classes. If teacher assignments are made based on seniority and not learners' needs, then the curriculum may be weakened by low morale and feelings of alienation among teachers and students.

The use of facilities, like the scheduling of instruction or the assignment of classes, is also an example of resource allocation. Often the assignment of classroom space is based on seniority, personal influence, or favoritism rather than need. Consider senior teachers who request and are assigned specific classrooms that are bothered by less outside noise, have better acoustics, better chairs, better lighting or closer proximity to the teachers' offices.

Other examples that might influence the success of a curriculum include the selection of instructional materials, and the availability and use of out-of-class resources and other support services. Money is also a major resource to adequately compensate the teachers and administrators for their time and effort.

Organizational Processes

Organizational processes refer to the way that resources interact together to support the curriculum. Three basic processes can be identified: communication, monitoring, and decision making.

1. The communication process includes the mode of communication and its flow within a program. Optional means of communication may entail posting messages on bulletin boards, distributing individual copies of messages through an internal (possibly electronic) mail system, and sharing information orally during meetings or between class breaks. The different modes of communication-oral and written-are usually present to some degree in every program, but the size of the program usually dictates the extent to which each is used.

   Flow of communication refers to the direction of communication in a program. The two major options for communication are vertical (from top to bottom or from bottom to top) and horizontal (teacher to teacher or student to student).

To illustrate the importance of communication for the successful implementation of a curriculum, imagine an intensive FL program in which teachers and administrators primarily use an Oral mode for communication. In this program, teachers are told their teaching assignments, and given their teaching schedules during staff meetings. Teachers are expected to communicate with each other in a horizontal direction to keep informed. With this kind of communication process, there is the ever-present possibility for incorrect information being spread. Obviously, this system is inadequate for large programs, and it can be a serious weakness even in small ones.

Another example is a FL program that distributes paper messages to all program participants. Not only is the distribution of paper expensive and contrary to conservation practices, the amount of paper can be so overwhelming that participants do not take note of high-priority messages.

Curriculum planners need to be aware of the options for communication within a program in order to design the most effective process of communication among its members.

2. The monitoring process entails a continual and systematic review of course implementation to determine how well the modification of curriculum goals meets the needs and expectations of the learners. Curriculum planners who wish to provide a learner-centered curriculum will devise processes for systematically revising the curriculum through regular monitoring and evaluation. This process might include

frequent surveys of student and staff opinions, analysis of test scores, and review of instructional materials.

3. The decision-making process refers to how decisions are made, who is involved in making them, and who implements them. In many FL programs, decision-making is equated with the administrative staff. While it is their task, it should not be done without input from the various participants in the curriculum. The more input that decision-makers have from teachers, students, secretarial support, parents/fee payers, and personnel in related programs, the more effective the decisions will be.

   Program units within the organization: In most FL curricula, and especially in intensive programs, there are several skill-based units. For example, intensive FL programs may have reading, writing, or listening programs. Some may have culture and study-skills programs and special-purposes programs, designed to teach the vocabulary and grammatical structures associated with a specific vocational area.

   The way these programs interact is of great importance to the effective achievement of curriculum goals. If priority is to be given to one or more programs, decisions should be based on the overall goals of the program, and not be the result of aggressive or weak leadership styles of the responsible administrators. Duplication can be avoided if the programs are planned in accordance with the overall curriculum goals and objectives.

   Communication among the different program units is another requirement for the success of a curriculum. Open communication among teachers and administrators involved in the different programs can help a FL curriculum achieve integrative goals. Open communication, encouraged by regularly scheduled meetings or discussions, workshops, and class visitations, can also instill feelings of cooperation rather than rivalry among teachers, administrators, and even students.

Planning an Effective Organizational Dimension

In order to assess the organization of an existing curriculum or plan for the effective operation of a new one, curriculum planners need to follow a systematic process. A systematic process for assessing and planning effective operations would include a thorough review and analysis of these major features.

A suggested model for assessing and/or planning effective foreign-language curriculum organization includes the following steps:

1. Review the curriculum goals and objectives.
2. Determine how to collect data in each area below:
   — resources
   — processes
   — programs
3. Collect and analyze the data.
4. Determine the procedures needing modification.
5. Develop a system for frequent monitoring of the organizational concerns for the continual improvement of the curriculum.

In order to follow the suggested model, curriculum planners should encourage participation from a number of teachers, administrators, and other support staff.

In the next step, the curriculum planning team should determine what kinds of data should be collected and how they should be gathered. Options for data collection include such direct methods as interviewing, observing, and holding discussions; indirect methods may call for reviewing and analyzing documents, observing the communication processes, and analyzing the goals and objectives of various skill-based programs within the overall program. The data collection activities should cover resources, processes, and programs.

Once the data are analyzed and interpreted, plans for effective and efficient organization should be designed and implemented. The final step of the model is the development of a system for frequent and systematic monitoring of the various organizational concerns.

6

Teaching English Writing

Writing, an important part of language learning, is essentially a reflective activity that requires enough time to think about the specific topic and to analyze and classify any background knowledge. Then, writers need suitable language to structure these ideas in the form of a coherent discourse. Our purpose, therefore, is to help our learners produce self-contained compositions. But for the learners to do so, they have to link and develop information, ideas, or arguments in logical sequences. Without writing practice, students have difficulty in achieving clarity, which is the goal of any writing exercise.

Too often we assume that after giving learners an initial stimulus to arouse interest in a given topic, we can simply leave them to complete the writing tasks. But even professional writers must make plans, use notes, reflect on issues, and make several rough drafts before completing their work. So, students who are still learning the process of thinking through writing require their teachers' help to structure and organize their ideas.

The Writing Task

Since letter writing is a part of the course, learners are already familiar with the letter format. We have selected the following task: Write a letter to your elder brother, persuading him to buy a television set for the family.

Objectives

Because we want the learners to write individually and enjoy writing, we start with the following objectives:

1. To integrate writing with speaking, listening, and reading.
2. To develop the strategy of persuasion and to reach a conclusion. Thus, writing is a tool for developing logical thinking.

The activity

Oral discussion, a "mind map," and a reading text are the pedagogical prompts to make writing a holistic activity. We begin by asking the learners to discuss the topic, in this case the advantages and disadvantages of having a television set at home. During this discussion a friendly atmosphere is built. Based on this information, the groups make their recommendations. This oral activity encourages brainstorming and exposes the learners to some new ideas. To ensure that the students have not left out facts, they are given a mind map and asked to predict what is in the text they will read. The facts and the mind map help students to come to certain conclusions. Learners are free to modify and expand their ideas based on the mind map, discussion, and text.

Operationalizing the Pedagogy

— *Step 1*: In groups of five, the students are given 10 minutes to discuss and write down the advantages and disadvantages of the topic. Then, one group gives the advantages, with input from the other groups, and another group is asked to give the disadvantages, with others adding their ideas. Both lists are put on the blackboard in the form of phrases or sentences. For example, our list of advantages and disadvantages for television in the home was as follows:

Advantages	Disadvantages
TV Programmes	TV violence stimulates aggressive behavior
Inform about current events	Violence leads the viewers to perceive the real world as more dangerous than it might be.
Fill up free time	Selection of program may cause conflict in the family
Provide access to new ideas	Watching TV becomes a habit and one loses the desire to create alternative forms of recreation
Educate	Watching TV breaks down communication within the family and social life suffers
Help to find career choices	Slang and catch words become active vocabulary

This activity gives the learners confidence in their abilities to create ideas and a sense of participation in their learning process.

— *Step* 2: The class is given a mind map to help them organize, expand, and clarify their ideas.

— *Step* 3: Next, learners read a given text related to the theme of the task. We select texts that provide information for the writing tasks. After learners have read the text we give them reading comprehension exercises, like true or false, main idea, and vocabulary development.

— *Step* 4: After students have identified some advantages and some disadvantages of the topic, we ask them to rearrange the main points so they can write two paragraphs. After five minutes, we circulate among the students to check their outlines.

— *Step 5*: Students are given 30 minutes to complete their letters, after which they check their own work for mistakes. Then they exchange papers to allow peer correction. They underline the errors and put the correct form in pencil. This gives them practice in correcting mistakes. Finally, we collect all the written work for the final correction.

Learning Words

Words are the basic unit of language form. Without a sufficient vocabulary, one cannot communicate effectively or express ideas. Having a limited vocabulary is also a barrier that prevents students from learning a foreign language. If learners do not know how to expand their vocabulary, they gradually lose interest in learning.

Vocabulary is taught mainly through reading. Each course book has a list of words with translations. Teachers must prepare extensively to master these words, and students try to memorize these words, unsure about which meanings should be remembered. The texts seem to be the only means of providing new vocabulary. As a result, learners forget words easily.

Learners seldom ask such questions as "What does run mean?" They know it is difficult to explain the meaning of a word without knowing the context. For example, look what happens to run in different contexts:

Don't run so fast.

She has a run in her stocking.

Soon there will be a run on the banks.

He batted in a run when it counted.

The car will run better now.

These sentences show that run may have different meanings. In fact, the word run appears not to change, only its surroundings change.

This function of context also applies to unfamiliar words. In expressing the idea of inferring meaning from context, Nuttall provides examples defining the word tock.

> She poured the water into a tock. Then, lifting the tock, she drank. Unfortunately, as she was setting it down again, the tock slipped from her hand and broke. Only the handle remained in one piece.

In this example, we see how context can help explain the meaning of an unfamiliar word.

Many professionals support the idea of inferring word meanings from contexts. Kruse suggests introducing vocabulary items in such a way as to allow the student to infer or guess the meanings from the context or illustrations. She believes that students should be encouraged to make intelligent guesses about word meanings. Clarke and Silberstein think students can often obtain a general understanding of an unfamiliar word if they continue reading.

Guessing word meaning from the context is possible. However, the question is whether it is also possible subjectively for students to be prepared to recognize and utilize the function of the context. In answering this, Twaddell analyzes the possibilities as follows: first, students know something about the content of the reading or listening materials from their knowledge of first language reading; secondly, they know how the meaning of the words they learn refers to parts of reality.

Since a contextual way of learning and expanding vocabulary is possible, we need to know how to train students in this skill. Nation gives a very good model on how to guess unknown words:

1. Look at the unknown word and decide its part of speech. Is it a noun, a verb, an adjective, or an adverb?
2. Look at the clause or sentence containing the unknown word. If the unknown word is a noun, what does this noun do, or what is done to it? And what adjectives describe it? What verb is it near? If it is a verb, what nouns does it go with? Is it modified by an adverb? If it is an adjective, what noun does it go with? If it is an adverb, what verb is it modifying?
3. Look at the relationship between the clause or sentence containing the unknown word and other sentences or paragraphs. Sometimes this relationship will be signaled by conjunctions like but, because, if, when, or by adverbs like however, as a result. The possible types of relationship include cause and effect, contrast, time, exemplification, and summary.
4. Use the knowledge you have gained from steps 1 to 3 to guess the meaning of the word.
5. Check if your guess is correct.
   (a) See that the part of speech of your guess is the same as the part of speech of the unknown word. If it is not the same, then something is wrong with your guess.
   (b) Replace the unknown word with your guess. If the sentence makes sense, your guess is probably correct.
   (c) Break the unknown word into its prefix, root, and suffix, if possible. If the meanings of the prefix and root correspond to your guess, it is good. If not, look at your guess again, but do not change anything if you feel reasonably certain about your guess.

Structural clues

We use structural clues to determine the type or grammatical category of the new word. This tells us the kind of meaning to infer or look for. For example, if students are told that kneaf is a verb, then the sequence, "the sploony urdle kneafed" will begin to make structural sense. Learners know that either sploony or urdle must be a noun, since their grammar knowledge tells them that a gap between the and a verb must be filled by a noun. Their morphological knowledge will tell them that sploony is probably an adjective, and if it is a noun, urdle may be another noun or an adverb. The teacher can provide students with practice in this technique by preparing specific exercises, like sentences containing nonsense words.

To help determine the meaning of words, the following clues are necessary: Students should learn to notice the various types of definition clues. Among these are the parentheses and footnotes, which are the most obvious definition clues. The meaning of a word can be explained in parentheses. For example: "We have adopted the view that every sentence can be described as a string (sequence) of constituents." Students can do exercises like drawing a line under the words in parentheses, or giving the meaning of the word that comes before the parentheses.

Most students enjoy learning words with similar and opposite meanings. The task is to get learners to recognize the definitional role these synonyms and antonyms often play. Students can learn that an unfamiliar word is often defined in a sentence using be and a synonym. For instance, a birthday party is an observance, that is, a remembrance of someone's day of birth.

Inference Clues

Inference clues require a higher level of analytical skill and practice than the previous types. For these types of clues, the same method of practice-recognizing elements and obtaining meaning from the elements can be used.

The meanings of the words can be inferred from examples, often by using physical clues such as i.e., e.g., and for example. Two sample sentences follow:

1. Iran is trying to restore many of its ancient monuments; Persepolis, for example, is being partly rebuilt by a group of Italian experts.
2. Perceiving, learning, and thinking are examples of cognitive processes.

By using the sum of the information in a sentence or paragraph, students can understand an unfamiliar word. Here are four examples:

1. Many products are sold to stop perspiration. This wetness comes from our body whenever we are too warm, work very hard, or are afraid, and it usually doesn't smell very good. (With a physical cue)
2. He's a really good athlete. He plays sports well. (Without a physical cue)
3. He's bound to win. He can't lose. (Opposite meaning)
4. The forsythia was covered with the golden flowers that bloom early in the spring. (Information given)

Readers can infer meanings of words by recalling similar situations or experiences and by making the appropriate inferences. Learners can often guess a word because it causes a result, or it is the result caused by something described in the text. One example follows:

> "The conflagration was so fierce that within just a few seconds one could see towering flames where the house had stood, and the smoke, which filled the sky, could be seen for miles around."

Sometimes learners can guess the meaning of a word by an explanation or a description given in the same sentence or paragraph:

> "The soldier was filled with intense remorse when he saw the terrible injuries suffered by people hit by the bomb his plane had dropped. He was ashamed to look at the bleeding and broken bodies as they were carried into the hospital. He cried and moaned when he saw that one was just a small child."

Students can learn a definition through the association between an object and its function or purpose for use: "The scientist removed the treatise from the shelf and began to read."

Many English words are formed using prefixes and suffixes. Teaching these meanings can help students decipher meanings of unknown words by analyzing the word's structure. Students can also practice forming words by using suffixes and prefixes.

Guessing

In developing the basic skill of guessing, Twaddell recommends that students practice while guided. "It is the teacher's task to organize the teaching so as to facilitate this development". Teachers should keep in mind that a certain amount of vagueness in guessing the meaning of words must be accepted. The teacher should not expect students to come up with exact meanings while guessing in this manner. Teachers should also help students to realize that "though successive encounters with a word and successive guessing in context after context, we sooner or later learn more and more precisely the meanings of the once unfamiliar word. By the time we have encountered a word often enough, the accumulated exclusions have subtracted enough from the vagueness, and the associations of the word with its meanings have become increasingly precise".

Teaching Creative Writing

There are several reasons to examine the processes of writing for English classrooms. First, contemporary critical, poststructuralist and genre theories have so emphasized the sociocultural constructedness of texts and meanings that the individual and the creativity of his or her textual constructions have all but vanished as meaningful concepts. Insofar as contemporary theory has infused our syllabuses, they're the less able to appreciate and allow for the individual and the creative. We certainly need to understand how what is personally experienced and expressed is also conditioned by aspects of our cultural context, including language. But we need also to go beyond truisms about those shaping contexts, to see how cultural products are also shaped by individuals, and how something of the personal remains, ineluctably, in these products.

Second, even when creative writing has been practised in English classrooms, it has very often been made subservient to reading, taking the form of "dependent authorship" or "transformation" of texts, often with an explicitly stated critical agenda. The point of such exercises is not the writing itself, but the understanding about the "base" text which this activity makes the more apparent. While such exercises may still permit the imagination to wander, its path is often pretty narrowly specified, and the problematic -these days usually a matter of politics or form - is generally determined by the teacher. This is not to deny that such activities may be valuable for students, in fostering their understanding of some of the processes of composition and the crafting involved in the making of both base text and dependent text. But these tasks allow little scope for invention outside their pre-specified conditions.

Third, in syllabi, teaching practice and assessment regimes, an impoverished version of "the writing process" has hardened into ritual. This entails one or more drafts, feedback on each, revision and editing, and "publication" of the "finished" product - often only in folios for the teacher's judgmental eyes. This orthodoxy can't do justice to the complexity of the processes that are actually involved. It concentrates on an aspect that's easier to manage in an English classroom: responding to drafts is familiar terrain for teachers, and the activity is reassuringly public, analytical, disciplinary and routine. But, as we shall see, it underplays other, more intuitive, creative elements in the development of a piece of writing that are harder to foster in classroom environments, and often can't be taught directly. Both aspects are needed in partnership.

This "psychic energy" can engage both the conscious, deliberative, rational and analytical activities of the mind and its intuitive, even unconscious sphere. Whether we call it intuition or the unconscious, this refers to those more diffuse mental activities that are a-logical, non-analytical, associative, intuitive, aesthetic and metaphoric. The undermind has some peculiar characteristics.

As is clear from the work of researchers like Csikszentmihalyi and others such as Claxton or Andreasen, who report on recent developments in cognitive science based on experimental studies into brain functioning, the undermind is at work in similar ways amongst creative people across a range of domains, from science, technology and mathematics to the arts and crafts, and even to interpersonal relations - though it will manifest itself differently in each domain, and perhaps to different degrees.

The older, "classic" literature on creative processes identified a number of components or "stages". These are preparation ("becoming immersed, consciously or not, in a set of problematic issues that are interesting and arouse curiosity"), incubation ("during which ideas churn around below the threshold of consciousness" - that is, in the undermind), insight, followed by evaluation of the "eureka" idea (for its practicability, its "fit" with the problematics, its elegance and the like) and the elaboration of the idea into a more fully worked out theory, plan or product. This theory is found wanting today, for two reasons: it misrepresents a complex, recursive process as a single, linear set of stages; and it focuses on the individual and underplays the influence of the domain of the endeavour and the field of expertise.

These concepts of the domain and the field in addition to the person are the contribution of Feldman, Csikszentmihalyi, and Gardner, based on their large-scale empirical research into creative individuals across a range of areas. They argue that we can't explain creativity by focusing just on individuals' processes; it also involves social, cultural and disciplinary contexts. If a person is to be creative, they must first be steeped in the domain of knowledge and practice that has preceded them and have mastered its constituent knowledge. Only then will they be in a position to innovate on what's been established in the domain. And after creation their products must be accepted by the field of experts, who act as gatekeepers to determine whether the creative idea, product or process will be accepted into the domain.

Creative Writing Processes

Dissonance

How do teachers and students identify a problematic that will offer the necessary "felt tension"? Teachers are rightly chary these days of inviting students to use creative writing as a confessional - and of course, most students are also reluctant to confide in their teachers as "Dear diary". Too often, instead, the problematic has been either narrowly defined by the teacher as a matter of form or left entirely open. It would be good if there were room within an English programme for students to be helped to look for the puzzle, conflict, tension, need or problem - in themselves, in their contexts, in what they're reading - that provides a felt tension. And then, to be allowed space and time to explore this, in a not too narrowly directed way. But classrooms are busy places that aren't very congenial to such introspective exploration. Often, then, teachers will take steps to kick-start students' inventiveness.

For instance, one way in which an artificial dissonance can be created is to draw up three columns on a page or board. In the first (the "Yes" column) a list of words (on the same topic) is brainstormed that are positive (for our purposes, it might be "intuition"). In the third (the "No column) a similar list of words is generated with negative connotations (for example, "institution"). The middle column is PO, short for possibilities (could "parody" be a way of being creative within a bureaucracy?). This kind of problem-solving is the first stage, which is then complicated by inventing a setting, two or three people and a couple of events, to create a story in which the shift occurs from the negative to positive pole (or vice versa) via the possibility.

The domain

Problematics in the domain can be of various kinds in creative writing. They may have to do with subject matter (what is usually represented, and how), with aspects of the structuring (how far a particular form may be pushed, until it breaks open into something else, for instance), with genre- and so on. Such domain-related dissonance moves the writer towards novelty - towards variation on the normative patterns, or at least on the patterns the particular artist has established.

All writers owe an enormous debt to their reading within and beyond their particular genre, and draw on it in their writing. Such intertextuality ranges from the unconscious echo, to the hardly perceptible gesture towards another text, to the conscious, deliberate homage or borrowing. In a real sense, we could not write if we had not read. This suggests that in the classroom students should be given opportunities to steep themselves in a range of imaginative texts, including film and other visual texts. And then be given opportunity to draw on these texts. Sometimes they may be undertaking "slavish" imitation, and at other times, they may be creating collages of text-fragments, or warping the given text in a parody. And in these acts of homage, they may see where there are limitations in the base text they want to go beyond, where there are opportunities for them to improvise on a melody or innovate more radically.

Situation

Classrooms are uniformly hostile to such loafing, which can perhaps occur properly only out of school. Is it possible create the classroom conditions conducive to the undermind with its more diffuse mental activities that are non-analytical, associative and metaphoric? Teachers might be able to prepare students indirectly for such states of mind, by now and then encouraging various forms of associative play with images and words and sounds, play that is "free" of "irritable reaching after" certain, "right" answers and outcomes.

Insight, Incubation, Generation

Two things are interesting here. One: it seems that the "head of steam" built up in the undermind by those catalytic events was so urgent that it could penetrate my consciousness - even through sleep. Note that the phrases are already that - words; but they also contain images, metaphors. In my experience, the intelligent unconscious can cast up on the shore of one's consciousness "pure" visual images not couched in words, or words alone, with or without an image attached or embedded in the words. The second point worth noting is that already at this stage, when the poem is only beginning to emerge.

Many teachers give students a form to write in. This is particularly the case with poetry in the junior grades, though of course the whole genre movement is predicated on such a procedure. Such structures can be useful, especially when students have little experience of the range of poetic forms from which to choose, or when they're overwhelmed by having too much crowding into view that clamours to be written about.

Then narrowing the aperture, through the discipline of form, can be enabling. However, when the demand to fill an empty form dominates the initial process, valuable insights, images, notions and expressions may never emerge. There should also be scope for writers to take rambling excursions over and under an idea without too early being required to rein in their words. Then, in conference, young writers can be helped to see what form may be latent in those words on the page, or may be brought in as a possible way of making the writing shapely.

These days the idea of a poet being "possessed" seems too romantic for words. Nonetheless, writers will talk of being taken over by their characters, or haunted by a poem they're composing. Of course we still remember to buy the bread and phone our mothers. It's rather like a tune you can't get out of your head: phrases resonate, sometimes submerged, sometimes drowning out other thoughts. Here it's a tune you're composing, often over an extended period, and this entails a sustained, if not continuous, attentiveness, which is a kind of commitment.

English curricula emphasise range in the writing students are to undertake. Teachers and systems want evidence of students' productivity across genres and contexts. And so the pressure is on for students to demonstrate their competence now in this text type, now in that, moving relentlessly on to the next due date. Certainly at times it can be useful for writers to be under pressure - it can catapult them into completing a piece of work. The risk is of bringing that piece to premature closure. It would be good if teachers could sometimes give students the scope to dwell in a piece of writing over a period of time, to return to it and play with it now and then, free of a looming deadline. Or to pick out a piece from their folios and read it afresh, as a reader not writer - and perhaps to see what the piece now needs.

"Workshop" books on writing poetry often present a variety of exercises and topics designed to open the door to the undermind. Many of these can be adapted for the classroom. They may not produce gems - that's not the only point - but they can be fun, and over time they can have the effect of lubricating the creaky hinges on that door. Other activities beyond writing can do similar work, such as visualising, or extemporizing role-plays and the like. Such exercises can be used in the initial stages, as part of the preparation and incubation that can generate insights and materials to work on.

Elaboration and Evaluation

It's one of the peculiar problematics of imaginative writing that its materials are words, their meanings worn so smooth in so many mouths. Our minds often trundle along wellworn tracks, carrying workaday thoughts dressed in grey pin-striped language. Conscious thought and the language that's integral to it work mostly in the realm of logic and deliberation, pressing towards the conclusiveness of a single coherent meaning.

It may well be harder - as many creative people have argued - to be original in propositions than in intuitions, or to unearth and question cultural assumptions that are embodied in the very way the wordscape is constructed. This problematic is also the challenge poets delight in: to make new patterns, new associations, new forms and meanings out of the threadbare materials of language. In this the undermind is a crucial partner to the uppermind.

The undermind isn't a realm of sublime inspiration that's always aesthetically impeccable. It offers material that's exuberant, richly associative, far-fetched, nonrational, even excessive; that's precisely its function and value. But in creating an aesthetic text, we move between the intuitive and the deliberative, between inner world and social world. For instance, the outer world provides my undermind with materials. The undermind performs its alchemy with these. The conscious mind can propose a problem for the undermind to work on, and so can to a limited degree direct its attention. The conscious mind evaluates and crafts what intuition offers. Some poets are content to use the materials thrown up by the undermind in pretty much their raw state, in order to evade the conscious mind's censorship.

Now the play of the undermind is fundamentally creative, but we can't say that the work of crafting undertaken by the uppermind is exclusively critical. That is, crafting is itself also creative: it involves making through (re)shaping.

There's often a fluid interchange between the critical/ evaluative and the creative/intuitive. A person who makes a creative contribution never just slogs through the long last stage of elaboration. This part of the process is constantly interrupted by periods of incubation and is punctuated by small epiphanies. Many fresh insights emerge as one is presumably just putting finishing touches on the initial insight.

These echo those earlier stutterings, but now serve up uncertain hope and reassurance. Perhaps it may help - if it's not daunting - for students to know that professional writers, who make their finished product look so simple and artless, often take their work through countless sometimes radical revisions, in which characters change, episodes arrive or depart, points of view and focus are radically modified - and so on.

Only those who are serious about their writing are likely to persist with the painstaking, patient work of planing and sanding. They may be few in any ordinary classroom. But it may be useful for those few, and perhaps others, to learn a few key things about crafting. Perhaps the first is that crafting involves more than editing. That is, the work needs to be seen as still provisional, still open to rethinking and radical redevelopment - even as the crafting moves towards realising its ultimate form and "argument". Such crafting involves work at different levels, from the merest detail to broad structuring. This work is of different kinds: it may entail cutting the words or details that have just come along for the ride; choosing more precise, fresh or appropriate words and phrases; or adding elements that will clarify or give needed emphasis. It may mean listening for the rhythms of phrasing or the patterns of assonance that have the right momentum and weight. It could mean shifting whole blocks of text around, to change the emotional emphases or narrative momentum and the like. In all this, intuition continues to play its part, though usually directed more by a more deliberate, analytic, aesthetic sense.

Most teachers know better than to attempt to get their students to do all this at once, on the same piece. Not that crafting should be taught in incremental, lock-step fashion, from detail to larger structures or the reverse: more experienced writers know how we shuttle between levels, and how change of one kind entails other changes. But a selective focus can be a sensible way to teach the various aspects of crafting over time. And of course, it should be clear that not all pieces must undergo the same exhaustive processes.

At times the teacher's demonstration on a sample piece can be useful, though it is sometimes of limited value unless it is sufficiently close to the pieces the students are working on, so that they can readily extrapolate and apply what's being modelled. Ideally, these things are best learned in a workshop situation, or one-on-one, where an experienced reader responds to the draft, helping the writer identify what needs development, coaching and - where appropriate - suggesting ways of crafting the text. This means encouraging the writer to decentre, to step out of the writer's shoes and into the reader's.

Engaging with the Field

The creative individual must reject the wisdom of the field, yet she must also incorporate its standards into a strict self-criticism. And for this one must learn to achieve the dialectical tension between involvement and detachment that is so characteristic of every creative process. Experienced writers have already internalised the eye and ear of their intended readeraudience: it contributes, paradoxically, to their sense of assurance. Even as they're drafting and crafting, they read and listen to the developing work as that reader would -evaluating the text in the light of that anticipated response, but not capitulating slavishly to what "the market" may want. Internalising the standards of the field has also meant much reading, over time - sometimes immersing oneself in others' work, giving oneself up to it, sometimes scrutinizing it closely to understand its workings.

Young writers are less likely to have developed that detachment, and this is where tactful intervention by the teacher is crucial: tactful, because it shouldn't overwhelm the student with either the impersonal authority of elders-and-betters or impose the teacher's personal authority and taste. The teacher needs to draw on her pedagogical judgment, to determine what feedback on what aspects of the piece will be most helpful at this stage of the work's and the writer's development. At times, it might mean the teacher simply suggests reading a particular poem or story that suggests a way of dealing with the problematic aspect of the draft.

Creative writing deconstructs in practice some of the binaries that operate in English curricula: between writing and reading; between on the one hand the concrete and particular in aesthetic texts and on the other the more general significance that hovers around those particulars; between deliberative, evaluative, critical intellect and intuition, conscious and unconscious; and between the received and the innovative. If creative writing appears to lean to one side of the equation here, that may be no bad thing, given the current tendency in much English education to reach for generalisations in reading and teach for analysis in writing. Creative writing offers a corrective, by enabling writers to know through practice the value of "metaphorical reasoning". English teachers and students may know something of this through reading aesthetic texts, and might know more of it through creative writing.

The imaginative, intuitive practices of language I've been discussing here are multifarious in their forms and irrepressible in their associative play. They liberate pleasure and energy through this play, and open those who practise creative writing to possibilities that deliberative, analytical thinking cannot engender or encompass - though as we have seen, such critical evaluative thinking is a necessary, complementary, productive partner.

7

Techniques of Teaching Reading

Students learning to read English as a foreign language find it a difficult process, and as a result, they do not enjoy it. Even if they are avid readers in their first language, as this teacher said many of her students were, all too often they do not become readers of English. We believe that reluctant readers can be reached and that they can develop a positive attitude toward reading in English. The first step is to consider the ways in which EFL reading is commonly taught. Traditional approaches and classroom practices, with their focus on translating, answering comprehension questions, or practicing skills such as finding main ideas, tend to ignore the larger context of students' attitudes toward reading and their motivation to read. The result, inevitably, is students with little or no interest in reading English. Yet students can discover the benefits and pleasures of being able to read in English. This can happen if extensive reading is incorporated into the EFL curriculum.

Extensive Reading Approach

The goal of an extensive reading approach is to get students to enjoy reading in the English language. It is an approach that sees reading not merely as translation or as a skill, but as an activity that someone chooses to do for a variety of personal, social, or academic reasons. The following is a list of characteristics of successful extensive reading programs.

1. Students read as much as possible, in class and outside of the class.
2. A variety of materials on a wide range of topics is available so as to encourage reading for different reasons and in different ways.
3. Students select what they want to read and have the freedom to stop reading material that fails to interest them.
4. The purposes of reading are usually related to pleasure, information, and general understanding and are determined by the nature of the material and the interests of the student.
5. Reading is its own reward. There are few or no follow-up exercises after reading.
6. Reading materials are well within the linguistic competence of the students in terms of vocabulary and grammar. Dictionaries are rarely used during reading because constantly stopping to look up words makes fluent reading difficult.
7. Reading is individual and silent. Student's read at their own pace, and outside class, they choose when and where to read.
8. Reading speed is usually faster rather than slower as students read books and other material they can easily understand.
9. Teachers orient students to the goals of the program, explain the methodology, keep track of what each

student reads, and guide students in getting the most out of the program.

10. The teacher is a role model for students—an active member of the classroom reading community who demonstrates what it means to be a reader and the rewards of being a reader.

Reading Materials

Getting EFL students to read extensively depends critically on what they read. The reading materials must be both easy and interesting. "Easy" means materials with vocabulary and grammar well within the students' linguistic competence. When students find no more than one or two difficult words on a page, the text is appropriately easy.

In our work with EFL teachers, we find that they are often reluctant to embrace the use of easy, high-interest materials. Even though the mix of difficult and boring materials can be deadly, teachers and students alike often appear to be under the spell of what might be called the macho maxim of reading instruction: no reading pain, no reading gain. This is unfortunate because struggling with difficult, dull material is not the way to become a willing EFL reader. Nor is it, in fact, the most efficient way of becoming an able reader.

Benefits of Extensive Reading

Reading a large amount of easy material has a vital role to play in learning to read fluently. Firstly, it helps wean students away from the word-by-word processing of text, encouraging them instead to go for the general meaning of what they read, and to ignore any details they do not fully understand. Secondly, by meeting the same patterns of letters, words, and combinations of words again and again, students process them more quickly and accurately, thus developing a sight vocabulary. Consequently, students increase their reading speed and confidence and can give more attention to working out the overall meaning of what they are reading.

In studies, extensive reading resulted in students' making significant gains in other aspects of foreign language competence such as listening, writing, and vocabulary. For example, in a study of university students who were failing their EFL classes, Mason and Krashen found that extensive reading helped the students improve their scores on a cloze test. Undoubtedly, part of the reason extensive reading has a positive effect on language learning is that it provides increased exposure to English.

The important role of comprehensible input in foreign language learning has been well documented by Krashen. But the impact of extensive reading may also be related to attitude. Many people find learning a foreign language difficult and feel more or less inadequate to the task. Successful foreign language reading experiences can counter such feelings of failure.

Materials Selection

The first task for teachers is to find materials that their students will find easy and interesting to read. If money is available, the task of assembling a wide selection of materials is relatively straightforward. When selecting reading materials for any age group and ability level, teachers must have the students' interests uppermost in mind.

High-intermediate and advanced students will probably enjoy reading carefully chosen English language books, newspapers, and magazines. A subscription to a local English language newspaper or one published internationally such as The International Herald Tribune or USA Today is sure to be appreciated by many students. General interest magazines such as People, with its celebrity interviews and gossip, or specialized magazines according to students' interests are also popular. If reading materials are in the students' fields of interest, comprehension is made easier because the students have knowledge of the subject matter.

For less advanced adult and adolescent learners of English, a useful source of reading material is books and magazines produced for native-speaking children and teenagers. Children's books, with big print and colorful illustrations, are relatively easy for EFL learners to read, and some have much to say to older learners. Best of all, they are short and can be read in a few minutes. Children's magazines are also worth investigating, as is popular teen literature. Both are often enjoyed by high-intermediate learners of all ages. Finally, comic books are beloved by all ages.

For beginning and intermediate students, however, the most suitable reading materials are books, magazines, and newspapers, especially those written for EFL learners. This literature is published in growing quantity, variety, and sophistication by both local and global publishers. There are hundreds of attractive fiction and nonfiction books appropriate to students of various ages and interests, including folk tales and science fiction, thrillers adapted from best-selling writers, classics, travel guides, and novels based on popular movies or TV shows.

Titles of books are listed in the catalogs of such publishers as Oxford University Press, Longman, and Heinemann. To make selection easier, the appendix of Day and Bamford includes a bibliography of 600 titles of high-quality language learner literature in English divided by student ability level.

When money is scarce, building a library is more difficult but not impossible. If the Internet can be accessed, it can be a source of extensive reading materials. Also, students can produce their own reading material. Students can dictate or write on topics of interest to them, and teachers can consult the students about rewriting, editing, and correcting. The finished products can be read by the rest of the class and by other classes, and the best can be kept in an ever-growing permanent library.

Cultural Considerations

Before introducing extensive reading in the classroom or for homework, the role of the students' culture must be taken into consideration. While reading is ultimately a solitary act by an individual, each culture has its own views of what reading is, and why and how it is done. Teaching in a "nonreading" culture, or in one that does not attach importance to reading for pleasure, makes the task of the EFL reading teacher more complex.

Orientation

Because students have become so accustomed to struggling through difficult English texts, a sudden plunge into a sea of simple and stimulating materials can be disorienting. It might not be obvious to serious-minded students, for example, why reading easy and interesting material should be a part of their EFL education. Nor do students necessarily know how to go about choosing and reading books on their own. It is therefore important for teachers to orient their students to the goals and methodology of an extensive reading program.

If appropriate, the orientation can begin by contrasting extensive reading with intensive or traditional kinds of reading instructions. The orientation should also include the ground rules of extensive reading:

— Select your reading materials based on your interests and reading ability.

— Do not use dictionaries.

— Practice the skills of either guessing at the meanings of unknown words or ignoring them.

— Do not be concerned with every detail. Keep reading in the face of difficulty and go for the overall meaning.

— If a book is boring or too hard, stop reading and find another book.

Such ideas capture the way that people usually read in cultures where reading is widespread. If students are from such a culture, telling them to approach EFL extensive reading in the same way as they read in their first language will make it clearer to them.

Extensive Reading and the Curriculum

Extensive reading can be blended into any EFL curriculum, regardless of the methodology or approach. For example, programs which utilize a reading-skills approach can add extensive reading without comprising the existing goals and objectives. Extensive reading complements a curriculum because it not only helps the program achieve its objectives of teaching students to read and pass examinations, but also it improves students' attitude toward achieving those objectives.

The ideal way to integrate extensive reading into the EFL curriculum is through a separate extensive reading course in which students read and report on their reading to the teacher and other students. However, for the majority of EFL situations, a new course is impossible since there is simply too much to do already. Alternatively, then, extensive reading can be included in the curriculum as part of an existing course, as a noncredit addition to a course, or as an extracurricular activity.

Incorporating a certain amount of extensive reading into a course already in the curriculum, regardless of the content of that course, is possible. This is done by adding a requirement that the students read a certain number of books per week or per semester. For example, in a grammar-translation class, the teacher can explain the benefits of extensive reading and how to go about it, and then explain the requirement such as reading one easy book per week and writing a short report on it.

Since class time is limited, most or all of the extensive reading would be done as homework. Reading a book of language learner literature takes between 20 minutes and two hours depending on the level of the book.

The teacher also can make sure students understand that they will be graded on or given credit for the extensive reading assignments. One way to grade students on their extensive reading is to set a scale of credit in relation to the amount they read. This could be done either in terms of books or number of pages read. For example, students who read 15 books a semester could have 15 points added to their final grade.

If there is simply no way-whatsoever that class or homework time can be given to extensive reading, a second possibility is for teachers to consider making it an optional part of their EFL courses. As an inducement to read, teachers could tell their students the rewards of extensive reading: for example, students will enjoy reading, their reading will improve, they will increase the size of their vocabulary, and so forth. The teacher would then encourage the students to read on their own, according to their interests and for enjoyment, and the teacher would keep a record of this reading. Students would need to understand that the extra reading is optional and not a formal part of the course. At the same time, teachers could consider giving extra credit that might influence a student's final grade.

A third possibility for adding extensive reading to an EFL program is through an extracurricular reading club. It could be organized and conducted like other extra activities. It would meet after school and be open to anyone taking EFL courses. A teacher would be in charge. A membership fee might be necessary if suitable reading materials are not available and need to be purchased. Having regular reading activities and goals helps create and sustain motivation and interest. For example, members might meet once or twice a week to give oral reports on books they have read individually. In addition, they might all read copies of the same book silently and individually, and then as a group, discuss it chapter by chapter and help each other with the meaning of difficult words. The club could also organize regular reading marathons in which each student aims to read a certain number of pages during a set period of time. A less structured form of a reading club is a reading/study lounge filled with attractively displayed English books.

A teacher can know if students are actually reading and that they understand what they read by having students answer questions. Another common way of checking reading is to require students to write a short summary of what they read. But however convenient such evaluations may be for the teacher, they tend to spoil the enjoyment of reading for students, reducing it to just another school activity. These common types of evaluation give no indication to the teacher of how much a student enjoyed reading. It is far more in the spirit of real-world reading for students to let the teacher or each other know what they felt personally about what they read. Students can write a paragraph or two about their reactions to a book. If the teacher has also read the same book, it will be obvious even from a student's brief comments if a book was read and how well it was understood.

Reaction reports are enjoyable for teachers to read because they give insights into students' thoughts and feelings. They also indicate to what extent a student is developing into an eager reader of English. If teachers respond to students' reaction reports with their own comments or questions, the reports help to establish a reading community in a way that answering comprehension questions and writing summaries never can.

Teachers can begin by reading some of the easy English books or other materials that their students are reading. This allows teachers to recommend books to individual students or to the whole class. Teachers might show students the cover and the title of a book and invite them to speculate on what the book is about. They can also tantalize students by pointing out and reading the cover blurb, the brief text that summarizes the story or introduces the book. Some students may not know how to choose an English language book that interests them, and this can be one way of teaching them how to go about it.

Whenever appropriate, teachers can read aloud to the students a paragraph from a book, a poem, a newspaper article, or an item from an Internet site. Teachers can post these and other interesting items on the classroom wall and invite students to do the same. In ways such as these, the teacher acts as a role model of a reader. Together with other incentives, like setting aside a special shelf for the most popular books in the class library and encouraging students to write book reviews for the school newspaper or draw posters for the school library, teachers can build a reading community with their students—a community of people who are enjoying and sharing English reading and are making it a part of their lives.

TEACHING FOR READING COMPREHENSION

Reading is the process of recognition, interpretation, and perception of written or printed material. Comprehension is the understanding of the meaning of the written material and covers the conscious strategies that lead to understanding. The process of reading deals with language form, while comprehension, the end product, deals with language content.

Reading is a process of communication from the writer to the reader. It involves the recognition of letters, words, phrases, and clauses, and in some respects, it can be considered a simpler process than comprehension. Comprehension, on the other hand, is a process of negotiating understanding between the reader and the writer. It is a more complex psychological process and includes linguistic factors, such as phonological, morphological, syntactic, and semantic elements, in addition to cognitive and emotional factors. The reader receives information from the author via the words, sentences, paragraphs, and so forth, and tries to understand the inner feelings of the writer.

As in grammatical analysis, distinctions between surface structures and deep structures also exist in semantic analysis. At the surface level, meaning can be classified into two broad categories: denotative meaning and connotative meaning. Denotative meaning is the meaning of words given in the dictionary and is "integral to the essential functioning of language in a way that other types of meaning are not". Connotative meaning is the communicative value of an expression by virtue of what it refers to, over and above its purely denotative meaning.

It reflects the real-world experience one associates with an expression.

In deep structure, meaning can also be divided into two categories: contextual meaning and pragmatic meaning. Unlike the surface meaning of a single word, contextual meaning is realized at the sentence level and is the meaning expressed by a sentence associated with its context. This type of meaning is not decided by the word itself but by the context in which the whole sentence functions. The pragmatic meaning is communicated in the feelings and attitudes of the writer. It is the writer's intended unspoken, or unwritten meaning.

In the reading process, the understanding of this type of meaning is implicative because this type of meaning lies outside the organization of language. It cannot be deduced from the linguistic system itself; it is realized at the functional level. Both contextual meaning and pragmatic meaning call for cognitive ability on the part of the reader. Thus, the distinction between surface structure meaning and deep structure meaning is that the former is the literal meaning while the latter is the inferential meaning.

Unfortunately, teaching RC in some schools focuses only on the surface structure level of comprehension and ignores comprehension at the deep structure level.

RC not only includes linguistic recognition and cognitive understanding (semantic comprehension at both surface and deep structure levels), but also tends to be affected by the reader's reactions to the content, which affect the reader's evaluation and appreciation, which become a part of the reader's RC. If there is no such evaluation and appreciation, comprehension will be incomplete.

With these preliminary considerations in mind, we need to attempt something new and more effective in teaching RC. The cognitive model presented here, adapted from Wallen's and Barrett's taxonomies, is so titled because it can be applied to students of different levels and adapted to their various needs.

Reading Comprehension Task Activities

The main aspects of activities associated with the cognitive model of RC strategies are described below.

Literal comprehension training

Training students in literal comprehension consists of using two types of tasks: recognition tasks and recall tasks. Recognition tasks require students to identify the main points in the reading selection or in exercises that use the explicit content of the reading selection. Recall tasks, on the other hand, demand that students produce from memory explicit statements from selections. Such tasks are often in the form of questions that teachers pose to students after reading the text. The difficulty level of these two tasks depends on various conditions, such as the students' linguistic abilities or needs and the number of events or incidents to be recalled. It is also believed that a recall task is more difficult than a recognition task when the two tasks deal with the same content.

Literal comprehension activities include:

a. *Recognition or recall of details:* identifying or recalling such facts as the names of characters, the time a story took place, the setting of a story, or an incident described in the story.

b. *Recognition or recall of the topic sentences/main ideas:* locating, identifying, or producing from memory an explicit statement or main idea from a selection

c. *Recognition or recall of sequence:* recalling the order of incidents or actions explicitly stated in the material

d. *Recognition or recall of descriptions:* identifying some similarities and differences in the text which are explicitly described by the author

e. *Recognition or recall of cause and effect relationships:* identifying reasons for certain incidents, events, or characters' actions explicitly stated in the selection

Inferential comprehension training

Students demonstrate their inferential abilities when they use their personal knowledge, intuition, and imagination as a basis for conjectures or hypotheses. Inferential comprehension involves more logical thinking than literal understanding and is elicited by teachers' questions which demand thinking and imagination. Some examples of inferential tasks are:

a. *Inferring supporting details:* guessing about additional facts the author might have included in the selection which would have made it more informative, interesting, or appealing

b. *Inferring the main idea:* providing the main idea, theme, or moral which is not explicitly stated in the selection

c. *Inferring consequence:* predicting what would happen in cause-effect relationships, or hypothesizing about alternative beginnings to a story if the author had not provided one, or predicting the ending of the story before reading it

d. *Inferring cause and effect relationships:* guessing what caused a certain event and explaining the rationale

e. *Inferring character traits:* hypothesizing about the nature of characters on the basis of explicit clues presented in the selection *f.* *Inferring figurative language:* inferring literal meaning from the author's figurative use of language

Evaluation

Students demonstrate evaluation when they make judgements about the content of a reading selection by comparing it with information provided by the teacher or authorities on the subject, or with their own experience, knowledge, or values related to the subject. Evaluation requires students to make judgements about the content of their readings based on accuracy, acceptability, worth, desirability, completeness, suitability, timeliness, quality, truthfulness, and probability of occurrence. The following are types of evaluation tasks:

a. *Objective evaluation:* judging the soundness of statements or events in the reading material based on external criteria, such as supporting evidence, reasons, and logic

b. *Subjective evaluation:* making judgements about the statements or events presented based on internal criteria, such as one's biases, beliefs, or preferences

c. *Judgements of adequacy or validity:* judging whether the author's treatment of a subject is accurate and complete when compared to other sources on that subject

d. *Judgements about appropriateness:* determining whether certain selections or parts of selections are relevant and contribute to resolving an issue or a problem

e. *Judgement of worth, desirability, or acceptability:* judging the suitability of a character's actions in a particular incident based on the reader's personal values

Appreciation

Appreciation deals with the psychological and aesthetic impact of the selection on the reader. It includes both knowledge of and emotional responses to literary techniques, forms, styles, and structures. Activities include the following:

a. *Personal impression:* reacting to the context, events, and characters

b. *Recognition of rhetorical devices:* identifying the rhetorical devices in the material and explaining their functions

c. *Reactions to the style:* describing and reacting to the writer's use of language and stylistic devices

d. *Evaluation of imagery:* identifying and assessing the effectiveness of the writer's sensory images

Advantages and practical value of the model

This model is designed for language teachers who train learners in RC. It has both theoretical and practical values. The advantages and special features of this model are summarized below:

1. The model is applicable at various skill levels and meets different needs. For example, it can be used in teaching literal meaning and concrete facts or deep structure meaning and literature appreciation.

2. It can be used to help students comprehend the text from different perspectives and to understand the implications of the content.

3. It enables students to analyze and summarize the text as well as to distinguish arguments from supporting details.

4. It enhances students' memorization and speed-reading.

5. Because students use different modes of thinking, it develops their critical thinking and inference skills.

6. Finally, it improves students' organizational skills and self expression.

Effective Reading Activities

In one current perspective on reading comprehension, the reading process is an interaction between a reader's prior knowledge and the information encoded in the text. The interactive model has recently been studied under the rubric of schema theory. This theoretical framework emphasizes that the reader is an active participant who can contribute to the construction of meaning. When reading, students interpret the text in light of their previous knowledge and simultaneously modify their original schemata as new information is learned.

From this perspective, there are two simultaneous and complementary ways of processing a text: top-down and bottom-up. In top-down processing, readers use their prior knowledge to make predictions about the text. In bottom-up processing, readers rely on their knowledge of language to recognize linguistic elements—letters, words, and sentence structure—for the construction of meaning. It is logical to suppose that readers must understand the individual parts of the text before they can grasp the overall meaning; but in practice, effective readers continually adopt a top-down approach to predict the probable theme and then move to the bottom-up approach to check their assumption by reading details. This implies that in teaching reading, teachers should instruct students to start their reading by using a top-down approach and later switch between the two approaches, as each kind of interpretation supports the other.

Many teaching techniques have been developed to activate students' prior knowledge for effective top-down processing in order to facilitate reading comprehension.

Several of them have been empirically proven to be helpful, but some have not. Surprisingly, prereading vocabulary exercises, despite widespread use, do not improve overall comprehension. In fact, vocabulary study may result in a word-by-word, bottom-up approach that is detrimental to comprehension. However, there are several activities that do help.

Semantic Map

The first activity that activates students' appropriate background knowledge of a given topic is the semantic map. The map is an organized arrangement of vocabulary concepts which reveals what students already know about the topic and provides them with a base upon which they can construct the new information learned from the text.

The teacher begins by telling students the topic they are going to read about and then asks them to make free associations with it. That is, students write down whatever words they think of when they hear the topic. Then the teacher asks students to group their associated words into categories and helps them label the categories. After reading the selection, the students may wish to revise the original map. The resulting map is the integration of students' pre-existing knowledge and their knowledge acquired from the text.

At first, students may have difficulty in categorizing free associations. The teacher can help them by conducting the discussion with the whole class. When students offer their associations, the teacher can list the responses on the chalkboard and discuss with the students how to put the associations into categories and what to label them. If there is more than one way to construct the relations among different concepts, the teacher may show students the different possibilities. This demonstration indicates how concepts can be organized around a topic.

After some illustrations, students can be divided into groups to carry out the discussion in teams. Interestingly, each group will usually come up with different versions, categories, and labels. The teacher may ask a representative from each group to draw the map on the chalkboard and decide if the concepts are appropriately constructed. From the demonstration, modeling, and discussion, students themselves will gradually learn how to categorize and label associations appropriately. The same procedure can be applied to the postreading discussion about revising the maps.

When generating associations, students are encouraged to look up new words in their dictionaries. The teacher may also consult a dictionary, preferably English-English, to help the students determine if the meaning and usage of new words fit the topic.

The following is a brief sample of a semantic map done by my students on the topic of North American Indians:

Hunting: buffalo, spear, bow and arrow

Lifestyle: nomad, riding horses, tent

Clothing: animal skin, long hair, feather

Ceremony: chief, dance, song, legend

Movie: *Dances with Wolves, Pocahontas*

Questioning

Another type of top-down processing activity is questioning. Questions may be generated by the teacher or by the students and should be done before the reading, rather than after the reading. Reutzel has proposed the Reconciled Reading Lesson to help teachers form effective prereading questions. Teachers who adopt the Reconciled

Reading Lesson reverse the textbook sequence by forming prereading questions from the comprehension questions that appear in the textbook after the reading selection or in the teachers' manual.

A problem in class is that not all the questions originally designed as post-reading exercises can be appropriately converted to prereading activities. For instance, a question like "What is the main idea of the second paragraph?" does not provide learners any clue to the content of the passage and fails to stimulate their prior knowledge which would enable them to make feasible predictions.

How do students generate text-related questions even before they read the passage? Williams gives an interesting three-phase approach to reading, with particular attention to the prereading phase. The approach begins by introducing the topic of the passage that students are going to read. Once the topic is presented, students are asked to work in groups and write a list in two columns. The first column lists things about the topic that they are sure of, and the second lists things that they are not sure of or don't know. See the list below for an example of what a list about whales might look like.

Table 1. Whale's List

Sure	Not Sure/Don't Know
1. Whales are not fish.	1. How many kinds?
2. The largest are 40 meters long.	2. How long do they live?
3. There are different kinds.	3. What do they eat?
4. They are used to make soap.	4. How fast can they swim?
	5. How heavy are they?

It is suggested that each member of the group in turn volunteer a fact or question, so that no group member is neglected. Afterwards, the teacher asks a representative from each group to write one or two items from their lists on the chalkboard so that some interesting items, which other groups may not have thought of, can be included.

In the reading phase, students are asked to read the text to verify what they were sure of and find the answers to questions they were not sure of. Using the list on the board, the teacher can ask students which sentences provide evidence for their responses.

In the postreading phase, the students are assigned tasks which consolidate their prior knowledge of the topic with information acquired from the text. For example, they may write an account of whales based on the information in their lists, or they may research the questions on their lists that have not been addressed in the text.

Williams' three-phrase approach provides an interesting way to activate students' prior knowledge and enhance their motivation to read. However, it has its practical limitations. For example, it may not be appropriate for opinion-giving text or fiction. It is best used with text that provides factual information. Furthermore, the length of the text should be moderate, because longer passages, which usually express more complicated concepts, may open too many possibilities for the students to question. As a result, the students may spend too much time generating questions in the prereading phase, and the list of questions may be too long to handle effectively. One possible solution to this problem is for the teacher to divide the text into sections and implement the approach section by section.

Another problem may occur when students generate statements and questions about the topic. This stage clearly requires a range of topic-related vocabulary and adequate writing competence. For the vocabulary problem, the same dictionary solution suggested for the semantic map can be adopted. When it comes to writing, if learners are not competent enough to produce correct sentences to reflect their ideas, they are allowed to write them in their native language. This writing does not focus on mechanics but gives priority to idea development for activating and developing background knowledge.

Previewing

The aim of previewing is to help readers predict or make some educated guesses about what is in the text and thus activate effective top-down processing for reading comprehension. Several stimuli in a text, such as the title, photographs, illustrations, or subtitles, are usually closely connected to the author's ideas and content. So, based on any of them, students can make predictions about the content of the text.

To make more specific predictions, however, students obviously need more guidance. The following guidelines can help:

1. Ask the students to read the title of the article. Do they know anything about this subject?
2. Have the students read the first few paragraphs, which generally introduce the topics discussed in the text. Can they determine the general themes of the text?
3. Then ask them to read the first sentence of each paragraph, usually the topic sentence, which gives the main idea of the paragraph. Can they determine the major points of the article?
4. Read the last paragraph, which often reveals the conclusion of the author. Have the students discuss how the author organizes the information to present his point of view.

The students then read the entire article for more detailed information. Since they already have an overview of the text, they can understand the rest of the information much more easily. The successful application of previewing depends on the presence of certain conventional features of English writing, namely, topic sentences and paragraphs of introduction and conclusion. However, not all kinds of texts have these rhetorical features.

Construct Validity in Reading Tests

Designing a good test is one of the most important tasks in teaching a reading course. The objective of this section is to provide guidelines to help teachers to write valid reading comprehension tests. To achieve this, some important areas from the reading and testing literature must be considered. The work of Goodman made important contributions to the way in which we understand reading today. He rejected the notion that reading is a precise process of perception and identification and described it as a psycholinguistic guessing game. He suggested that the reader begins a reading task already possessing certain information, which allows her/him to pick up important fragments of the text in order to reconstruct it. The information that readers already possess is characterized as background knowledge.

Schema Theory

The importance of background knowledge in reading is also central to schema theory. This theory claims that reading a text implies an interaction between the reader's background knowledge and the text itself. The knowledge that is organized and stored in the reader's mind is called schemata. According to this theory, fluent readers relate their schemata with the new information present in text.

Many teachers now accept the view that reading is the result of a two-way communication between the reader and the text, achieved through the simultaneous interaction of bottom-up information processing (which involves word recognition, sound/spelling correspondence, etc.,) and top-down processing.

Construct Validity in Testing

Validity is an important factor in designing good reading comprehension tests. Psychometricians distinguish between several types of validity. Savignon mentions five: face validity, content validity, predictive validity, concurrent validity, and construct validity.

Construct validity explores the adequacy of a test in relation to theory. In the case of reading comprehension, tests should reflect the theoretical assumptions under which reading teachers operate. For instance, if teachers view reading as an interactive process, tests have to be designed to give students opportunities to make use of their schematic knowledge.

Carrell distinguished between formal schemata (knowledge about the structural configuration of texts) and content schemata (knowledge about the subject matter of text). She found that a reader may fail to understand a text if it does not follow a formal schema (coherent organization) or if content schema was lacking. Carrell and Alderson and Urquhart documented the discipline-specific effect of content schemata in their work with students who found it difficult to read texts which did not relate to their area of study. Stefensen, Joagdev and Anderson found that a particular content schema may not exist for a reader if that schema is culturally specific; so the texts used in a test should be culturally accessible. Rivers suggested that the cultural link between culture and language must be maintained to allow for complete understanding. Thus, previous cultural and schematic knowledge is a factor in constructing reading comprehension tests.

Rumelhart claims that bottom-up and top-down processing occur simultaneously while reading. This reading process should not be neglected in tests. A test should not concentrate solely on asking students to draw inferences from a text. The test should also allow for the reader's use of lower level decoding skills. Briefly put, tests should contain items that test both, bottom-up and top-down elements.

Tests should provide sufficient room for students to use their background knowledge. Shing and Dunkel investigating EFL listening comprehension, suggest that the passage-dependent items (listening-bound items) and passage-independent items (information related to the listener's prior knowledge) should be balanced. Eliminating passage-independent items would leave only low-level questions on the tests, reducing the chance for the listeners to make inferences and predictions while processing the aural information. On the other hand, if passage-dependent items are skipped, the test will draw primarily upon background knowledge and not measure listening skills. This testing implication of Shing and Dunkel's work is applicable to reading-comprehension tests.

Guidelines for Constructing Valid Reading Comprehension tests

Based upon this body of research, we suggest the following guidelines for constructing reading tests.

— Reading tests should take into account the students' content schemata by including texts about topics which have been dealt with previously in class.

— Reading tests should not include texts which are tied to a culture.

— Tests should contain passage-dependent, as well as passage-independent items.

— The texts should be coherently organized to allow students to draw the organizational patterns from their formal schemata.

— It is advisable to use texts which are semantically complete and authentic.

— The tasks involved in answering test items should allow for higher-level interpretation skills, as well as low level recognition skills.

— These guidelines reflect the latest developments in the area of reading research within the framework of schema theory.

8

Vocabulary Learning

Vocabulary learning is usually incorporated into other classes, especially reading. In these classes, words may be defined only in passing or students may engage in more traditional individual exercises such as filling in blanks or matching words and definitions. These activities are not enough for effective word learning. She describes a study she did which indicated that interactive and communicative vocabulary activities can lead to better word learning. Students in the study had a separate vocabulary class that met three hours per week and used a vocabulary-building textbook. Students also read self-selected and assigned reading passages and engaged in activities that required them to use the vocabulary words they were learning while interacting with one another. These students performed significantly better on a posttest than students in a control group.

Boyd Zimmerman outlines three important assumptions of her study:

1. Word learning is a complex task.
2. Some word learning occurs incidentally as a result of context-rich activities such as reading.

3. Word knowledge involves a range of skills, and word learning is facilitated by approaches that provide varied experiences (i.e., with reading, writing, speaking, and listening).

The first assumption is important for teachers to acknowledge and for students to understand. Students realize the important role vocabulary acquisition plays in all aspects of their language learning, but few have really thought about what it means to learn a vocabulary item. On the student information sheet that our students fill out at the beginning of the semester, we typically ask our high-intermediate and advanced students how many words they think the class should learn each week. Answers typically range from 10 to 200 words. The next class period, we spend time brainstorming together about what it means to learn a vocabulary word. We ask them, "How do you know when you've really learned a word?" Once they think about it, they usually identify all the major aspects of word learning: part of speech, pronunciation, meaning(s), register, connotations, spelling, grammatical usage, context, and so forth. After our discussion, we again ask them how many words they think they can learn each week. Usually the students revise their estimate to a more realistic level.

The second assumption relates to the source of vocabulary items. In our reading classes, we do not always use separate vocabulary builders. Instead, the words on our vocabulary lists come from the context of the reading passages and discussions about them. Words that are new for all or most students make the vocabulary lists. At lower levels, teachers may fill in a set to complete the list. For example, if the word senior is used in an article about colleges, a teacher may add the words freshman, sophomore, and junior to complete the set. At upper levels, teachers may add words that are opposites or are close in meaning; for instance, if covert comes up in an article, overt might be added.

The third assumption is that learning will be enhanced by giving students various types of activities with the words. It is not enough to do just one activity with a word. Students must learn about the words in a variety of interactive ways.

Boyd Zimmerman's study set out the following parameters for teachers who would design the interactive vocabulary lessons. In her subjects' special vocabulary classes, each lesson was to include the following:

1. multiple exposures to words;
2. exposures to words in meaningful contexts;
3. rich and varied information about each word;
4. establishment of ties between instructed words, student experience, and prior knowledge; and
5. active participation by students in the learning process.

While reading teachers may not have time to include all of these elements in a single lesson, keeping them in mind can help in creating interactive lessons. For example, using a computer search of a newspaper or magazine on the Internet can yield a word used in several contexts. Students can often learn much about a word's usage from seeing it in various contexts. This activity would cover both parameters one and two. Parameter five is particularly important to keep in mind; the students must be active, not passive, learners.

Interactive Vocabulary Activities

Interactive vocabulary activities can be designed to fulfill any of the following purposes:

a. Exposure (our interpretation of Boyd Zimmerman's concept of clarifying "word meaning and illustrate appropriate usage")

b. Expansion (our interpretation of her concept of "using the appropriate word form in context")

c. Expression (our interpretation of the concept of demonstrating "word knowledge in either oral or written original expression using the target words")

While each of the three purposes should be covered at each level of language proficiency, the proportion of class time spent on activities for each purpose will vary according to the level of the students. We have found that at beginning levels, we tend to spend more time clarifying the meaning or exposing students to the words and refining usage. At the intermediate level, we spend a lot of time refining and expanding as well as expressing the word. At the high-intermediate and advanced levels, we find students can work on the first two purposes more independently, and this allows more opportunities for them to practice expressing themselves using the target words in class.

Beginning-level Exercises and Activities

At the beginning levels of language and vocabulary acquisition, we address the problems of English language learners with very limited vocabularies—perhaps recognition of only 100 to 200 English words and, often, production control of far fewer words. Leaving aside the difficulties of defining precisely what it means to know a word, we realize that recognition of even 800 to 1,000 English words limits students to the reading of simple, usually adapted materials. For students at these very beginning levels of language and vocabulary instruction, recognition of and exposure to English words are critical.

Thus, many of the vocabulary activities we recommend focus on beginners.

1. Discrete Point Recognition of Differences (Exposure)

One very basic exercise is to train students to spot differences between words that are similar in appearance but often radically different in terms of grammar and/or meaning. Often, elementary readers do not notice these distinctions and are processing (or trying to process) text using the wrong semantic element. The teacher should anticipate these difficulties and make students aware of the micro-level at which they must initially process these items.

Exercise:

Directions: Cross out the word that is different:

1.	dairy	dairy	daily	dairy
2.	butter	better	better	better
3.	quite	quite	quite	quiet

While the initial exercise is usually done in writing, the simple act of checking answers in class can provide an oral production exercise that also helps students associate what they see with what they hear.

2 Semantic Framing (Exposure/Expansion/Expression)

At the lowest levels of vocabulary instruction, we feel it is also important to provide a semantic frame for vocabulary words that are part of a larger schema. Some examples of these are levels of education (freshman, sophomore, junior, senior; primary, secondary, undergraduate, graduate), foods (meats, vegetables, fruits) or kinds of books (reference, fiction, nonfiction). Again, because we are presupposing that, for the most part, students do not have these completed frames, the first task of the teacher is to provide them. This presentation can also form the basis for further practice or testing.

Exercise A:

Animal	Meat (general)	Meat (specific)
Pig	Pork	bacon, ham, sausage
Cow	Beef	hamburger
Chicken	Chicken or Poultry	
Duck	Duck or Poultry	
Turkey	Turkey or Poultry	
Sheep	Mutton	
Lamb	Lamb	

In this example, the teacher has discretion in whether she chooses to introduce poultry or even drumstick, thigh, or wing. But the student starts to see a system as well as the refinement of some basic vocabulary items, such as using pork instead of pig. The following exercise can help beginning students practice what they've just learned. Students can explain why they have chosen to eliminate the word they did. For example, in number one below, beef is not an animal but a kind of meat.

Exercise B:

Directions: Cross out the word that doesn't belong in the same group.

1.	pig	chicken	beef	sheep
2.	bacon	ham	sausage	pig
3.	elementary	junior	freshman	senior

While our focus is still on recognition at the elementary levels, a teacher can do a simple production exercise, again using a chart. In a framing exercise such as this, not only the vocabulary is being emphasized but also the ways in which items can be organized. Teachers should be prepared for alternate configurations and the students' explanations for why they see the system as they do.

3 Grammatical Charting of New Word Forms (Expansion)

Along similar lines, making grammatical distinctions among vocabulary items at the lowest levels is also a useful reading and vocabulary skill. Teaching students to use their rudimentary knowledge of a word to extrapolate to a word family is a valuable skill. Many students recognize and understand the word different but are unaware of the verb differ. Many textbooks attempt to treat this issue in one of two ways. Often, the text will provide a part-of-speech chart, and ask the student to complete the chart, such as the following:

Exercise A

Noun	Verb	Adjective	Adverb
difference	—	—	—
national	—	—	—

Sometimes, especially in highly contrived texts, the reading actually contains all (or most) of these word forms, but more often, it does not. Without a reading context from which to draw these items, the student is usually left to dictionary work, which may or may not be successful at this level. The texts may attempt to teach students to generate these forms from their knowledge of suffixes.

At the beginning levels of English language instruction, we prefer that students keep a running chart of new words based on previously learned vocabulary and complete the chart as they actually encounter these new forms. This focus on recognition in natural occurrences has two advantages. It helps students learn word forms by allowing them repeated exposure over time. It also prevents the problem of over generalizing, for example, looking too long for the adjective form of disappear or generating friendly as an adverb. Production of words may be most appropriate for intermediate or advanced levels of students who are more familiar with the morphological forms.

As lower-level students gain an appreciation of new words and the families they belong to, it may be useful to have students produce sentences, initially in writing, which highlight their understanding of the different parts.

Exercise B

Directions: Write short sentences, using each of the following words. Use only one of the words in each sentence.

n. happiness	n. friend	n. diet
adj. happy	adj. friendly	v. diet
adv. happily		adj. dietary

Note that an exercise like this has several advantages. It demonstrates that not all word families have the same members, that is, there is not always an adjective or adverb form. Also, even at this simple level, students can be exposed to some of the irregularities of English. For instance, -ly is not exclusively an adverbial ending, and sometimes the noun and verb or the noun and adjective are the same. By providing the appropriate form, the teacher keeps the student from the over generalizing errors noted above. It should also be noted here that in the example above, discretion has been exercised in not introducing befriend at the elementary level. This is a judgment call and is completely within the teacher's purview as the most knowledgeable assessor of her own students' abilities.

4 Oral Production (Expression)

Finally, at all levels but especially at the elementary level, helping students make the connections between how new words appear and how they sound is an important part of vocabulary instruction. While we are not advocating pronunciation exercises per se as part of the reading curriculum, it is important for learners to hear as well as see new vocabulary. For that reason, in exercise 1 above, the teacher could also use oral exercises or combine oral with written input in having students find the differences between minimal pairs. Similarly, the sentence production exercise noted above could be done orally in class.

Intermediate-level Exercises

If beginning levels of reading and vocabulary instruction are characterized by recognition, then perhaps a useful way of looking at intermediate instruction is through the lens of refinement and expansion. While the elementary-level student is grasping for a word to communicate meaning, the intermediate student is seeking to expand that basic vocabulary.

For example, while a beginning-level student learns that elementary school is the first level of formal education, the intermediate student may learn that grammar school, primary school, and grade school are other ways of characterizing this same concept. To give another example, the teachers may be satisfied if a beginning student learns the word thin. At the intermediate level, however, the student may be ready to go on to learn the new words slim or skinny as well as their connotations.

1 Differentiating Related Vocabulary Items within a Set (Expansion)

Exercise

Directions: Give an example of a food that can be described by each of the following adjectives.

sweet	bland	bitter	pickled
salty	tasteless	spicy	rich
sour	plain	hot	heavy

Note that this vocabulary application exercise could be completed before, during, or after a reading about food. As a prereading exercise, it not only provides a more complete frame for talking about foods, but allows students to assess which words they already have in their individual vocabularies and which ones they must add. It also allows for refinement of vocabulary by having students apply their understanding of a given word. For example, is rice tasteless? If so, why or why not? Is a lemon sour or bitter? How about an orange? Do students need to learn tangy? These kinds of exercises generate practice in a context that requires them to fine-tune their knowledge and learn more about the nature of vocabulary acquisition.

2 Application Questions (Expansion)

Another application exercise that allows students to expand a basic vocabulary is preparing lists. For example, having read an article in which terms such as symbol, motto, and oath occur (and are defined within a given context), students are asked to apply their understanding of these terms.

Exercise

1. List three entities that might have a motto.
2. List three symbols and what they represent.

3. List three situations in which you might be asked to take an oath.
4. List three different kinds of ceremony.

They must not only distinguish between similar constructs—a symbol versus a motto—but they must also apply their definition of each term in a new and different context. Thus, students are exposed to a number of attributes about the various vocabulary items they have encountered in the reading text. Item 4 may provide an opportunity for further refinement; many intermediate and advanced students confuse ceremony and celebration because they are used in overlapping contexts.

3 Generating Sets (Expression)

A production exercise that can also be used to help students examine and practice their schema for certain constructs is an adaptation of the commercial game Outburst. In the commercial version, one team of players gets a card with 10 preselected items that fit into a category, and the other team has 60 seconds to guess which items that fit the category are on the list. For example, the card might read "Countries beginning with the letter C" or "Harrison Ford movies." The guessing team gets points for every match they make within the 60 seconds. Teams alternate and points are totaled after the game is complete.

With this exercise, we almost always begin with teacher-generated categories, and the students complete the lists of items. Later on, we modify these cultural categories to ones which correlate with new vocabulary, such as academic majors or Olympic sports, and have one team of students generate the lists themselves. Then, the other team is given the category and creates a list or guesses the items listed by the first team. All students get to practice vocabulary in a specific frame.

Exercise

After reading a unit on recreation, for example, have teams of students create cards for "Things you can do at the beach" or "Equipment you need for camping." Give teams five minutes to generate the cards. Then allow the opposite team to guess what is on the card. This provides multiple exposures to the specific vocabulary and the larger frame to which those vocabulary items belong.

4 New Context Prompts (Expansion/Expression)

A final example of an intermediate-level exercise that helps students expand and refine vocabulary is applying a set of vocabulary items to a completely new context. For example, consider some of the vocabulary associated with a disaster:

survivors	crashed	serious
fatalities	destroyed	fatal
injuries	tallied	miscalculated
consequences	investigated	tragic

If students have read an article about an airplane crash, the teacher can ask them to write a news article about a natural disaster or even the misuse of a recalled drug. Students can also be assigned to describe the events depicted in photographs of a rescue attempt, avalanche, or earthquake. When using old frames in new ways, students practice expression and expansion of vocabulary terms.

Advanced-level Exercises and Activities

After vocabulary words are gathered from reading passages and put on a list, students at the high-intermediate and advanced levels can find most of the basic information about the words using a good English-

English dictionary at home. At the beginning of the semester, we spend a little more class time going over parts of speech, the meaning of each word in the context of our reading passage versus other meanings the word might have, and what we call related word forms (noun form, verb form, etc.). In class, we quickly go over this information together. Students also bring questions about synonyms and make notes about connotations or register given in their dictionaries. During discussion, we can clarify the subtle differences between synonyms, such as aggressive/assertive, and contexts in which each word might be used.

The new words advanced students encounter usually do not fall into neat sets or frames. In addition, new words are often used less frequently than words students may have studied at lower levels. For example, one high-intermediate reading passage yielded the following new words:

to long for	deceptive	mentality
broke	to halt	to land in

Even if they are avid readers, students could wait quite some time for another opportunity to encounter these words. Therefore, students at this level need opportunities to practice using words on their vocabulary lists so that they will feel more confident using the words independently later. These activities also allow students to further refine their knowledge of word usage. We try to include both oral and written activities with each set of words, with the written work preceding the oral work.

1 Web Contexts (Exposure)

This activity can be done by students or the teacher. The activity is similar to Grammar Safari in that the class can examine several contexts in which the vocabulary words are used. Find an online magazine or newspaper that is searchable. Type in the vocabulary word and copy the sentence(s) in which the word is used. These sentences can be copied into a word processor or posted on a web page. Be sure to note the source of each sentence. Students can see the words used in different contexts.

An example of a web site using this technique was developed by one of the authors and contains examples of the word evolved from sources such as the Smithsonian, The Christian Science Monitor, and the local campus newspaper.

2 Pre-paraphrasing (Expansion)

At the high-intermediate and advanced levels of reading and writing, we spend a lot of time working on paraphrasing. Part of good paraphrasing is changing the grammatical structure of a sentence, but students can also benefit from a vocabulary activity that challenges them to use different forms of the vocabulary words.

This activity can be done with sentences from the reading passages, teacher-generated examples, web contexts, or even student-generated sentences from activities such as 3 below. Sentences must be chosen with care because this activity will not work with all words.

Example:

This type of paint can tolerate extremely hot temperature; therefore, it is very popular in places like Arizona. (change to tolerant)

3 Finish the Sentence (Expression/Expansion)

Students are given the beginning of a sentence and asked to complete it in a way that clearly shows they know the meaning of the word. Students will need some examples to help them understand the concept of clearly showing they know the meaning. Here is a simple example using a nonsense word, slibdaty:

> *He was slibdaty, so I gave him some soup.*
>
> *He was slibdaty, so I gave him some soup and told him to get some rest and see the doctor the next day.*

In the first sentence, the meaning of slibdaty is not clear; in fact, most people would probably guess hungry. In the second sentence it is clear that slibdaty means sick. Ask students for similar sentences using new vocabulary.

Examples:

a. Mark is such a vindictive person that his dislike for Margaret soon evolved into ________________.

b. We decided to choose another venue for the concert, so ________________.

After students write their completions, the other students and the teacher can check them and give feedback about whether or not the completion clearly shows the meaning of the word. Grammatical usage problems may also surface here and can be refined. Other students can give suggestions for improvement or propose alternative completions.

4 Stories and Role-plays (Expression/Expansion)

One way students can demonstrate word knowledge is to use several of their vocabulary words in a single context. Working in pairs in class allows students to discuss the vocabulary items together in an effort to use them correctly. This can be done at several levels, in writing or orally.

Exercise A

Using as many words as possible from a vocabulary list about capital punishment (e.g., premeditated, guilty, disposable), write a newspaper account or police report of the murder described in Edgar Allan Poe's story The Tell-Tale Heart.

Exercise B

With a partner, use the words below to write a paragraph, story, or news report.

question	hassle	master	mentality
cost	deceptive	long	appraisal
impulsive	broke	land	halt
assess	*hectic	*foster	*prolonged
*contemplate	*mandatory		*void

(*to recycle from a former vocabulary list)

Exercise C

Write a dialogue using one of the groups of words and phrases from the list below.

1. extravagant	flamboyant	spurn
2. perceptive	whitewash	farfetched
3. self-reliant	savvy	spur on
4. stumble on	out of the blue	intuitive

5. Real-life Questions (Expression)

In small groups, students draw questions from a bag. Each question contains a vocabulary word or words. Students are allowed a few minutes to think and then must read their question out loud and answer it using the vocabulary word or a related form. Other students in the group listen to see if a vocabulary word is used and if it is used correctly. In more advanced classes, other group members can be encouraged or required to answer each question after the first person.

Word Wall Approach

Research that has focused on vocabulary learning can guide teachers in planning explicit vocabulary instruction. For the purposes of this chapter, we focus on three research findings of particular relevance to language classroom settings. First, research has demonstrated that vocabulary learning requires multiple exposures to new lexical items in various discourse contexts. Multiple exposures, of varying intensities and in diverse contexts, are said to gradually lead to a large recognition vocabulary.

Some researchers claim that a minimum of 10 to 12 exposures is needed for learners to begin to see the range of meanings and uses for new lexical items. Duquette and Painchaud assert that "lexical competence is progressively constructed by the repeated occurrence of a word within a variety of new contexts." Claims such as these suggest that teachers should consider the ways in which they systematically recycle important vocabulary in the classroom.

Second, research has revealed that elaborated vocabulary learning occurs when students make meaningful connections between new and already familiar words. Instructional approaches that juxtapose new and known words allow students to use known words in new contexts, with new nuances, new meanings, and new collocations and to use new words with practical associations. This expanded sense of new and known words allows for faster processing of semantically related words.

Third, research has shown that context can be a powerful influence on students' vocabulary growth. But learning words from context is a long-term process during which word meanings are slowly accumulated through exposure and learning. By means of explicit instruction, language teachers can "compress that process so that students can learn more words in a shorter period of time". Key here is the need to focus instructional attention on words that students have encountered in rich contexts, rather than from decontextualized word lists.

The Word Wall approach, expanded upon in the remainder of this chapter, easily accommodates the three principles of vocabulary learning that were just introduced. As will become evident, the Word Wall provides opportunities for multiple exposures to lexical items; it encourages students to make connections between new and known words; and it can be used in response to meaningful contexts or to build relevant context around new words. Equally important, the Word Wall promotes active student involvement, a key to effective learning in general.

The Word Wall approach was originally designed to challenge and motivate high-achieving as well as reluctant first language students (in elementary and secondary classrooms) to develop vocabulary learning skills and to internalize new vocabulary. Using a set of six word-filled wall panels, each with a different background color corresponding to a different curricular objective (e.g., phonic elements, word form classes, grammatical forms, or spelling patterns), Green literally surrounded his students with words. The ever-present "walls of words" became an integral part of his classroom. Each panel included lexical items selected from vocabulary lists corresponding to classroom readers and lists of high-frequency English words.

The walls of words were not used as the only instructional tool for vocabulary development in his classroom, Green also integrated them into various classroom lessons, accommodating individual, pair, small group, and whole class instruction. Students consulted the Word Wall as a thesaurus and spell-check during writing assignments; they used it as a resource during language development lessons, and they often turned to the Word Wall for rainy-day lunch and recess activities.

Specific lessons and competitive games were devised around the Word Wall to encourage the development of vocabulary learning strategies and to build students' vocabularies through explicit instruction, implicit learning, multiple exposures, and opportunities for making meaningful connections among words. The repetition and recycling made possible by using the Word Wall approach, and the possibility for students to see, touch, hear, say, and write the words, resulted in greater vocabulary retention and an enthusiasm for learning vocabulary.

Green's Word Wall approach can be adapted for a range of L2 instructional settings without sacrificing its commitment to vocabulary development. The flexibility of the approach makes it easily adaptable for settings where space considerations, curricular priorities, student motivation, and student needs may require changes in procedure.

Adaptations in five areas are worth pointing out. First, Green used multiple walls, devoting each one to a particular language objective. Limited classroom wall space may determine how the basic approach is realized in other instructional settings. In our intensive English program, we used one full wall of our classroom for the Word Wall, placing paper word strips on the carpeted wall with small pieces of self-adhesive Velcro.

In other classrooms, an unused blackboard, the space above a chalkboard, a bulletin board, sheets of butcher paper, or portable poster boardmay be most useful for teachers who do not have exclusive use of a classroom. The poster board could serve as the background for lexical items. Regardless of how words are actually displayed, what is important is that words be added gradually and remain easily visible to all students.

Second, Green's use of colors to distinguish one Word Wall from another can also be adapted for diverse classroom settings. Each of Green's walls had a different background color, each color corresponding to a separate language goal; for example, words on the blue panel highlighted certain spelling conventions, and words on the orange panel depicted certain phonics rules. If only one wall is available, individual lexical items, rather than the wall itself, can be color coded.

Depending on curricular goals and student needs, the colors used might correspond to specific word classes, such as green for nouns, blue for verbs, orange for adjectives, and yellow for adverbs. Colors could also correspond to different thematic units, for example, violet for words first encountered in a unit on pollution and red for words encountered in a unit on endangered species. Colors might also be used to identify the curricular component in which the new lexical item was first introduced, like tan for words encountered in a reading class and pink for words introduced in a listening class. We implemented the latter approach, using separate colors for lexical items first encountered in our core content-based course (pink), reading lab (green), video course (yellow), and TOEFL preparation course (blue). These color designations triggered associations in our students' minds about the place and time they first encountered the word, thereby facilitating word recognition and use.

A third adaptation to Green's approach relates to the types of exercises used with the Word Wall lexicon. The use of phonics and an emphasis on spelling patterns may not be appropriate for all instructional settings. Thus, teachers will need to devise activities that meet the vocabulary learning needs of their own students. For example, some teachers may want to focus on synonyms and antonyms, word order, collocations, and semantic groupings to reinforce vocabulary building and introduce students to vocabulary learning strategies.

The fourth adaptation deals with choice of lexical items for the Word Wall. Green selected words from formal word lists and then placed them on his various Word Wall panels. Lexical items can also be selected directly from the "texts" that students are exposed to in class, interpreted broadly to mean all sources of content information including readings, videos, charts and graphs, lectures, and so forth. In our opinion, lexical items that students have encountered (or are going to encounter) in real texts, for authentic communicative purposes, are the best candidates for the Word Wall. The contextualized exposure and realization that the word is important are likely to assist students in learning the vocabulary item and connecting it to other words encountered in other texts and on the Word Wall.

Furthermore, there is no need to restrict selection decisions to the teacher alone. In fact, involving students actively in lexical item selection has many benefits. When students are given the chance to select words for the Word Wall, they often develop a sense of ownership toward the Word Wall and its contents. The act of selecting a Word Wall entry often leads to multiple exposures to the word as a result of deliberate decision-making and negotiations with classmates.

Teachers can devise any number of explicit instructional activities and games to make use of the Word

Wall itself and the lexical items placed on the Word Wall. Curricular priorities and student needs will determine, in large part, the nature of the activities integrated into the classroom. It can be assumed that students will make reference to the Word Wall at other times, on their own, when editing their written work, when engaged in problem-solving activities, when reading, and so forth. The incidental learning that takes place as a result of the ever-present Word Wall is likely to contribute to students' vocabulary learning.

We describe here a small sampling of Word Wall activities that can be integrated into L2 instruction to promote vocabulary learning and to support language skills development. Some of these activities require very little class time, whereas others can become part of more substantive lessons. What is important to remember is that each encounter with a word from the Word Wall and its meaning will contribute to students' growing understanding of a word and the many contexts in which it can be used. For ease of presentation, we have divided the sample activities below into three categories based on their primary focus: explicit vocabulary building, reading and writing, and speaking and listening.

Explicit Vocabulary Building Activities

The Word Wall can be used for explicit vocabulary building in numerous ways. The activities described below represent a fraction of the options that teachers have to assist students in developing their vocabulary. Many traditional vocabulary-building activities can be adapted and used with the Word Wall.

— *Word clustering*. The creative movement and reorganization of lexical items on the Word Wall will help students make connections between new and known items as well as semantically related words.

Examples of creative groupings include clusters of topically related lexical items, pairs of logically linked adjectives and nouns, pairs of synonyms and antonyms, groups of words from the same word class, semantic groupings, and lexical linkages that are simply playful.

— *Multiple meaning awareness activities.* Students can be asked to find Word Wall items with more than one meaning. In pairs or groups, students can be asked to write sentences that demonstrate the different meanings of the word or to write definitions.

— *Vocabulary expansion.* The teacher identifies a useful word, which is likely to be unfamiliar to most students, that is repeated throughout a reading passage. The teacher defines the word and then puts it on the Word Wall. Students scan the reading passage for the word and highlight it throughout the passage. The class then discusses other contexts in which the word might appear.

— *Word part exercise.* After teaching students about word parts, the teacher directs students to find words on the Word Wall that have identifiable word parts. The teacher asks questions to determine if students can define the words using their knowledge of word parts.

— *Matching.* After distributing Word Wall entries to all students in class, students circulate to find classmates who have synonyms, antonyms, or words in the same word class. As a possible variation, half of the students can be given strips with definitions of Word Wall items, and the other half can be given the actual words. Students circulate to match words and definitions.

— *Finding synonyms or antonyms.* The teacher generates a set of sentences with synonyms or antonyms of

Word Wall entries underlined. Students must replace the underlined word with its counterpart from the Word Wall.

— *Crossword puzzles.* Using lexical items from the Word Wall, the teacher creates a crossword puzzle. Definitions can be used as clues, or sentences with blanks can be used if context clues lead students to the solution.

Reading and Writing Activities

Vocabulary building is often associated with reading and writing instruction. The sample activities described below illustrate three ways in which teachers can integrate the Word Wall into reading and writing instruction.

— *Cloze passage.* The teacher (or students) creates a cloze passage with blanks for Word Wall items. Students attempt to fill in the blanks with appropriate words from the Word Wall.

— *Free writes/speed writes.* Students can be asked to write for a certain length of time, incorporating a designated number of lexical items from the Word Wall into their writing. The teacher may assign a topic or leave it open. As a variation, teachers can ask students to incorporate Word Wall items into poetry writing, class newspaper articles, or other written assignments.

— *Journal entry.* Students pick a lexical item from the Word Wall and write a journal entry about it. For example, a student can pick the word compassion and write an entry about a compassionate acquaintance.

Speaking and Listening Activities

New vocabulary items can easily be integrated into speaking and listening activities to promote vocabulary growth through meaningful use and recycling. The Word

Wall activities described below depict some of the options that teachers can choose from.

— *Descriptions.* Students describe a classmate or classroom object by using Word Wall items. Students can play a game in which they use five words from the Word Wall to describe something or someone in the room while other students try to identify the person or item being described.

— *Guessing game.* In pairs, one student describes a Word Wall entry (i.e., how it is used or its definition) and the student's partner tries to match the clue with a Word Wall item.

— *Story telling.* The whole class tells a story. The teacher models the process by starting the story, including several Word Wall items in the introduction, and pointing to the words on the Word Wall when they are used. A student volunteer builds upon the story line until a designated number of Word Wall entries has been used, and then the story is continued by other students.

— *Twenty questions.* The teacher chooses a word from the Word Wall, and the students guess it by asking the teacher up to 20 yes-or no-questions.

— *Word Wall Jeopardy.* The teacher chooses various words from the Word Wall and places them in categories, such as nouns, adjectives, or content words. Then the teacher supplies definitions to students in "Jeopardy" game-show fashion. Teams of students try to identify the appropriate Word Wall match. The group with the highest number of points wins.

Guidelines for Word Wall Use

During our initial attempts at integrating a Word Wall into

our EAP curriculum, we encountered some minor stumbling blocks. We list the most noteworthy problems and follow that with guidelines that can facilitate the integration of the Word Wall concept into other L2 classrooms.

1. Too many lexical items were placed on the Word Wall during our first semester using the Word Wall. There was simply not enough time to recycle all the Word Wall items into classroom activities so that the words could be retained. Consequently, many items placed on the Word Wall were never revisited or recycled. Thus, at the end of the first semester, many of the Word Wall items were still fairly unfamiliar to students.

2. When students began to select words for the Word Wall, they sometimes chose uncommon or infrequently used words, thereby placing words on the Wall that would have little value for them.

3. Words were placed on the Word Wall uncreatively, most often in orderly horizontal and vertical lines.

4. Initially we restricted Word Wall choices to single words rather than common phrases, idioms, phrasal verbs, or fixed expressions, severely limiting student exposure to other relevant and useful vocabulary.

In response to these problems, we generated a list of guidelines that assisted us in using the Word Wall more effectively during the second semester. We offer the following eight suggestions to help L2 teachers use the Word Wall with ease.

1. Whether lexical items are selected by teachers or students, three criteria need to be met before words are placed on the Wall: The Word Wall entries must be useful to the students, usable by the students, and

frequently used by native speakers. Without establishing such criteria, students might select lexical items that are infrequently used or archaic. Teachers should be able to reject words that do not fall into these categories. To remind students of these criteria, teachers might want to place a small, but conspicuous flyer on the Word Wall.

2. Lexical items that stem from contextualized exposure, rather than a decontextualized word list, are the best candidates for the Word Wall. Posting words that students need to understand to comprehend a reading, a chart or graph, a video, a lecture, a bulletin board display, or a guest speaker is an effective Word Wall strategy.

3. Teachers should consider how many words that they want on the Word Wall at any given time and over the course of a term. At the beginning of any term, the Word Wall will be empty. Over time, as students encounter more new words as a result of exposure to new texts, new lexical items will be chosen for Word Wall placement. In some settings, teachers may choose to rotate words, dating all entries and keeping them on the Wall for a few weeks or for the duration of a specific instructional unit. In other settings, students can vote on the words they want to keep up or take down. Some sort of procedure needs to be established to maintain the flow of words on and off the Word Wall. What is critical, however, is the need to keep entries on the Wall long enough to ensure that students have multiple encounters with the words and opportunities to make connections between new and old entries.

4. Word Wall selections need not be confined to single words. Phrases, idioms, fixed expressions, and phrasal

verbs should be included if deemed important for the students.

5. Word Wall items should be placed creatively rather than in straight, orderly rows on the Word Wall. Teachers and students alike should be willing to move Word Wall entries around on the Wall. Fixed placements limit the usefulness and versatility of the Wall for instructional purposes. Activities that encourage students to move words about reinforce multiple usages and collocations.

6. The Word Wall is most effective when it is "a regular and predictable part of classroom activities." It should therefore become a physical presence in the classroom early in the term and a standard instructional tool shortly thereafter.

7. A variety of instructional activities that recycle and review Word Wall items should be devised for classroom use. The physical placement of lexical items on the Word Wall is just the beginning. The Word Wall entries should be incorporated into subsequent speaking, listening, reading, writing, and grammar activities.

8. Depending on student age, maturity, and language proficiency, teachers must decide how to introduce the Word Wall concept. Simply involving students with the ever-present Wall so they develop a noticeable degree of comfort with many lexical items on the Wall can serve as an adequate introduction in some settings. More explicit commentary on vocabulary learning strategies might be appropriate in other classrooms.

9

Games for English Classrooms

Language learning is a hard task which can sometimes be frustrating. Constant effort is required to understand, produce and manipulate the target language. Well-chosen games are invaluable as they give students a break and at the same time allow students to practice language skills. Games are highly motivating since they are amusing and at the same time challenging. Furthermore, they employ meaningful and useful language in real contexts. they also encourage and increase cooperation.

Creative Games for the Language Class

There is a common perception that all learning should be serious and solemn in nature, and that if one is having fun and there is hilarity and laughter, then it is not really learning. This is a misconception. It is possible to learn a language as well as enjoy oneself at the same time. One of the best ways of doing this is through games.

There are many advantages of using games in the classroom:

— Games are a welcome break from the usual routine of the language class.

— They are motivating and challenging.

— Learning a language requires a great deal of effort. Games help students to make and sustain the effort of learning.

— Games provide language practice in the various skills-speaking, writing, listening and reading.

— They encourage students to interact and communicate.

— They create a meaningful context for language use.

Many of us in the teaching profession use games occasionally in the classroom. Most of us are familiar with some of the more popular language games such as "Twenty Questions," "The Whispering Game," "Making a Sentence," "Asking Yes/No Questions" or "Kim's Game."

Just A Minute

The first game is called "Just a Minute" and it is adapted from a radio game show broadcast over the British Broadcasting Corporation (BBC). It was aired over the BBC many years ago and was highly entertaining. This is how you play the game:

1. Divide your students into groups. Get each group to give themselves a name.
2. The objective of each group is to get as many points as possible.
3. The task is to speak on a topic for a minute. The referee (the teacher) will provide the topics.
4. The competition-members of the other groups-should try to "wrestle" the topic away from the person who is speaking on it. There are three ways to do this:

   — *Hesitation*: When a student pauses for too long a break, it is considered a hesitation.

— *Repetition:* When a student keeps repeating a particular word or phrase, it is considered repetition.

— *Deviation:* When a student digresses, he can be faulted for deviation.

5. A timekeeper will ring the bell once the minute is up. The person who is speaking when the bell rings will win 10 points.
6. The group with the most points is the winner.
7. The teacher should determine the topics based upon the students' level of proficiency. Some examples of topics are:

   — My Childhood

   — My Family

   — My Favourite Things

   — Ghosts

   — My Ideal Partner

   — Teenagers

   — A Country I'd Like to Visit

   — My Favourite Food

   — If I Had Three Wishes, I'd Like . . .

The choice of topics would also depend on what is being taught in the lesson for the day. For example, if the teacher is conducting a lesson on describing people and places, s/he could provide topics such as My Mother, Someone I Admire, A Teacher I'll Never Forget, My Hometown, or My School.

This game is particularly suitable for teaching oral communication skills. It is also useful as a pre-writing or pre- reading activity. It can be effectively utilised when teaching topics such as describing, narrating, expressing viewpoints, agreeing, disagreeing, and describing procedures.

Win, Lose, or Draw

The second game is quite a well-known one. It is currently being aired on television in Malaysia, and is called "Win, Lose, or Draw." You can play it with as many teams as you like, preferably keeping it to a maximum of four or five teams.

Instead of giving the students the words to draw, I find it even more effective if you get the students to concoct the words themselves. The words should be "drawable," not too easy nor too difficult. Give the groups about 10-15 minutes to come up with the words; then the teacher should go round to the different groups to check out the words. Tick out those that are suitable and try and offer alternatives for those words that you consider unsuitable. Each topic should then be written out on a small piece of paper which can be rolled or folded up. Then, collect all the topics and place them in separate boxes in front of you.

The game is then played as follows:

— Divide your class into groups.

— Start with the first group. A member of the group should come to the front of the classroom and pick out a piece of paper containing a topic given by members of the other groups. S/he then has to draw the topic on the blackboard once the timekeeper gives the "begin" signal.

— Appoint someone to keep time. A student has a maximum of 60 seconds to draw the object. This can vary according to your students' abilities.

— The objective is to try to score as few points as possible.

— The task is for group members to try to guess what the student is drawing in as little time as possible.

— The student doing the drawing cannot talk, make any sound, nor act out the word. Only when his/her group members have guessed the word correctly, can s/he indicate or gesticulate that they have done so.

— The teacher has to be alert and listen carefully whilst the students try to guess what their friend is drawing. Once they have guessed the topic correctly, the teacher stops the action.

— The timekeeper announces the time taken and records it on the board.

— After this, the next group takes its turn. The game can be played for many rounds. Students in each group should take turns drawing.

— At the end of the game, the scores are tallied. The group with the fewest points is the winner.

Games For Vocabulary Presentation and Revision

Vocabulary acquisition is increasingly viewed as crucial to language acquisition. However, there is much disagreement as to the effectiveness of different approaches for presenting vocabulary items. Moreover, learning vocabulary is often perceived as a tedious and laborious process.

There are numerous techniques concerned with vocabulary presentation. However, there are a few things that have to be remembered irrespective of the way new lexical items are presented. If teachers want students to remember new vocabulary, it needs to be learnt in context, practised, and then revised to prevent students from forgetting. Teachers must make sure students have understood the new words, which will be remembered better if introduced in a "memorable way". Bearing all this in mind, teachers have to remember to employ a variety of techniques for new vocabulary presentation and revision.

Gairns and Redman suggest the following types of vocabulary presentation techniques:

— *Visual techniques.* These pertain to visual memory, which is considered especially helpful with vocabulary retention. Learners remember better the material that has been presented by means of visual aids. Visual techniques lend themselves well to presenting concrete items of vocabulary-nouns; many are also helpful in conveying meanings of verbs and adjectives. They help students associate presented material in a meaningful way and incorporate it into their system of language values.

— *Verbal explanation.* This pertains to the use of illustrative situations, synonymy, opposites, scales, definition and categories .

— *Use of dictionaries.* Using a dictionary is another technique of finding out meanings of unfamiliar words and expressions. Students can make use of a variety of dictionaries: bilingual, monolingual, pictorial, thesauri, and the like. As French Allen perceives them, dictionaries are "passports to independence," and using them is one of the student-centered learning activities.

Using Games

The advantages of using games. Many experienced textbook and methodology manuals writers have argued that games are not just time-filling activities but have a great educational value. W. R. Lee holds that most language games make learners use the language instead of thinking about learning the correct forms. He also says that games should be treated as central not peripheral to the foreign language teaching programme.

A similar opinion is expressed by Richard-Amato, who believes games to be fun but warns against overlooking their pedagogical value, particularly in foreign language teaching. There are many advantages of using games. "Games can lower anxiety, thus making the acquisition of input more likely".

They are highly motivating and entertaining, and they can give shy students more opportunity to express their opinions and feelings. They also enable learners to acquire new experiences within a foreign language which are not always possible during a typical lesson. Furthermore, to quote Richard-Amato, they, "add diversion to the regular classroom activities," break the ice, "[but also] they are used to introduce new ideas".

In the easy, relaxed atmosphere which is created by using games, students remember things faster and better. S. M. Silvers says many teachers are enthusiastic about using games as "a teaching device," yet they often perceive games as mere time-fillers, "a break from the monotony of drilling" or frivolous activities. He also claims that many teachers often overlook the fact that in a relaxed atmosphere, real learning takes place, and students use the language they have been exposed to and have practised earlier. Further support comes from Zdybiewska, who believes games to be a good way of practising language, for they provide a model of what learners will use the language for in real life in the future.

Games encourage, entertain, teach, and promote fluency. If not for any of these reasons, they should be used just because they help students see beauty in a foreign language and not just problems that at times seem overwhelming.

Choosing Appropriate Games

There are many factors to consider while discussing games, one of which is appropriacy. Teachers should be very careful about choosing games if they want to make them profitable for the learning process. If games are to bring desired results, they must correspond to either the student's level, or age, or to the material that is to be introduced or practised. Not all games are appropriate for all students irrespective of their age.

Different age groups require various topics, materials, and modes of games. For example, children benefit most from games which require moving around, imitating a model, competing between groups and the like. Furthermore, structural games that practise or reinforce a certain grammatical aspect of language have to relate to students' abilities and prior knowledge. Games become difficult when the task or the topic is unsuitable or outside the student's experience.

Another factor influencing the choice of a game is its length and the time necessary for its completion. Many games have a time limit, but according to Siek-Piskozub, the teacher can either allocate more or less time depending on the students' level, the number of people in a group, or the knowledge of the rules of a game etc.

When to Use Games

Games are often used as short warm-up activities or when there is some time left at the end of a lesson. Yet, as Lee observes, a game "should not be regarded as a marginal activity filling in odd moments when the teacher and class have nothing better to do". Games ought to be at the heart of teaching foreign languages. Rixon suggests that games be used at all stages of the lesson, provided that they are suitable and carefully chosen. At different stages of the lesson, the teacher's aims connected with a game may vary:

— *Presentation.* Provide a good model making its meaning clear;

— *Controlled practise.* Elicit good imitation of new language and appropriate responses;

— *Communicative prastice.* Give students a chance to use the language.

Games also lend themselves well to revision exercises helping learners recall material in a pleasant, entertaining way. All authors referred to in this article agree that even if games resulted only in noise and entertained students, they are still worth paying attention to and implementing in the classroom since they motivate learners, promote communicative competence, and generate fluency. However, can they be more successful for presentation and revision than other techniques? The following part of this article is an attempt at finding the answer to this question.

Use of games for presenting and revising vocabulary

Vocabulary presentation. After the teacher chooses what items to teach, Haycraft suggests following certain guidelines. These include teaching the vocabulary "in spoken form first" to prevent students from pronouncing the words in the form they are written, placing the new items in context, and revising them. A number of techniques can be adopted to present new vocabulary items. The presentation of new vocabulary is classified according to verbal and visual techniques following Gairns and Redman's classification. Among visual techniques are flashcards, photographs and pictures, wall charts, blackboard drawings, word pictures, incongruous visuals, realia, mime, and gesture. Students can label pictures or objects or perform an action.

Verbal techniques consist of using illustrative situations, descriptions, synonyms and antonyms, scales, and, as described by Nation, using various forms of definition: definition by demonstration (visual definition), definition by abstraction, contextual definitions, and definition by translation. Allen and Valette also suggest the use of categories-organising words into sets, subclasses and subcategories often aided by visual presentation. Those learners who are more autonomous can make use of other techniques such as asking others to explain the meaning of an unknown item, guessing from context or using either of a variety of dictionaries.

Description of the groups. For the purpose of vocabulary presentation, we chose two groups of third form students. With one of them we used a presentation game and with the other translation and context guessing. In both groups, students' abilities varied-ranging from those whose command of English was very good, able to communicate easily using a wide range of vocabulary and grammatical structures, and those who found it difficult to communicate. The choice of lexical items to be introduced.

Description of vocabulary picture-puzzle. To prepare the puzzle, we cut two equal-sized pieces of cardboard paper into rectangles. The selected idioms were written onto the rectangles in the puzzle-pieces board and their definitions on the game board. On the reverse side of the puzzle-pieces board, we glued colorful photographs of landscapes and then cut the puzzle-pieces board into individual pieces, each with an idiom on it. The important thing was the distribution of the idioms and their definitions on the boards. The definitions were placed in the same horizontal row opposite to the idioms so that when put together face to face each idiom faced its definition.

Puzzle Pieces Board. The idioms and their definitions were the following:

— to be soft in the head: *foolish, not very intelligent;*

— to have one's hair stand on end: *to be terrified;*

— to be two-faced: *to agree with a person to his face but disagree with him behind his back;*

— to make a face: *to make a grimace which may express disgust, anger;*

— to be all eyes: *to be very attentive;*

— to be an eye-opener: *to be a revelation;*

— to be nosy: *to be inquisitive, to ask too many questions;*

— to be led by the nose: *to be completely dominated by, totally influenced by;*

— long ears: *an inquisitive person who is always asking too many questions;*

— to be all ears: *to listen very attentively;*

— to be wet behind the ears: *to be naive, inexperienced;*

— a loose mouth: *an indiscrete person;*

— one's lips are sealed: *to be obliged to keep a secret;*

— to have a sweet tooth: *to have a liking for sweet food, sugar, honey, ice cream, etc.;*

— to grind one's teeth: *to express one's fury;*

— to hold one's tongue: *to say nothing, to be discrete;*

The task for students. Work out the puzzle by matching the idioms and their definitions. First, put puzzle-pieces on the desk with the word facing up. Take one and match the idiom to the definition. Having done that, place the puzzle-piece, word-side-up, in the chosen rectangle. When you have used up all the pieces, turn them over. If they form a picture of a landscape, the choices are correct. If not, rearrange the picture and check the idiom-definition correspondences.

The game objectives. To work out the puzzle, students had to match idioms with their definitions. The objective of the game was for each pair to cooperate in completing the activity successfully in order to expand their vocabulary with, in this case, colloquial expressions. All students were active and enjoyed the activity. Some of their comments were as follows: "Very interesting and motivating" "Learning can be a lot of fun" etc. Students also had to find the appropriate matches in the shortest time possible to beat other participating groups. The element of competition among the groups made them concentrate and think intensively.

Translation activity. The other group of students had to work out the meanings of the idioms by means of translation. Unlike the previously described group, they did not know the definitions. The expressions were listed on the board, and students tried to guess their proper meanings giving different options. My role was to direct them to those that were appropriate. Students translated the idioms into Polish and endeavored to find similar or corresponding expressions in their mother tongue. Unlike the game used for the purpose of idiom introduction, this activity did not require the preparation of any aids. Fewer learners participated actively or enthusiastically in this lesson and most did not show great interest in the activity.

Revising vocabulary

Many sources referred to in this article emphasise the importance of vocabulary revision. This process aims at helping students acquire active, productive vocabularies. Students need to practise regularly what they have learnt; otherwise, the material will fade away. Teachers can resort to many techniques for vocabulary consolidation and revision. To begin with, a choice of graphs and grids can be used. Students may give a definition of a given item to be found by other students.

Multiple choice and gap filling exercises will activate the vocabulary while students select the appropriate response. Teachers can use lists of synonyms or antonyms to be matched, sentences to be paraphrased, or just some words or expressions in context to be substituted by synonymous expressions. Doing cloze tests will show students' understanding of a passage, its organisation, and determine the choice of lexical items.

Visual aids can be of great help with revision. Pictures, photographs, or drawings can facilitate the consolidation of both individual words as well as idioms, phrases and structures. There is also a large variety of word games that are "useful for practising and revising vocabulary after it has been introduced". Numerous puzzles, word squares, crosswords, etc., are useful especially for pair or group work.

Description of the group. A questionnaire is given to teachers to determine their view of using games for vocabulary teaching. In response to the questionnaire, many teachers said they often used games for vocabulary revision. Some claimed they were successful and usually more effective than other methods.

The crossword puzzle. After completing a unit about Van Gogh, students wanted to expand their vocabulary with words connected with art. The students compiled lists of words, which they had learnt. In order to revise the vocabulary, one of the groups had to work out the crossword puzzle.

Students worked in pairs. One person in each pair was provided with part A of the crossword puzzle and the other with part B. The students' task was to fill in their part of the puzzle with the missing words known to their partner. To complete the activity, learners had to ask each other for the explanations, definitions, or examples to arrive at the appropriate answers. Only after getting the answer right could they put it down in the suitable place of their part of the crossword. Having completed the puzzle, students were supposed to find out what word was formed from the letters found in the shaded squares.

Students enjoyed the activity very much and did not resort to translation at any point. They used various strategies to successfully convey the meanings of the words in question-e.g., definitions, association techniques, and examples. When everyone was ready, the answers were checked and students were asked to give examples of definitions, explanations, etc., they had used to get the missing words.

10

Strorytelling

Storytelling is the original form of teaching. There are still societies in which it is the only form of teaching. Though attempts have been made to imitate or update it, like the electronic storytelling of television, live oral storytelling will never go out of fashion. A simple narrative will always be the cornerstone of the art of teaching.

In dealing with stories, learners have an experience with the powerful real language of personal communication, not the usual "teacherese" of the foreign-language classroom. Colloquial or literary, unaffected or flowery-the full range of language is present in stories. Oral stories develop listening skills in aunique way. The listeners benefit from observing non-polished speech created on-the-spot.

While listening to stories, children develop a sense of structure that will later help them to understand the more complex stories of literature. In fact, stories are the oldest form of literature.

Through traditional tales, people express their values, fears, hopes, and dreams. Oral stories are a direct expression of a literary and cultural heritage; and through them that heritage is appreciated, understood, and kept alive.

Stories in Affective Realm

Through a story, listeners experience a vicarious feeling for the past and a oneness with various cultures of the present as they gain insight into the motives and patterns of human behavior. However, many storytellers feel that cognitive enrichment is not the primary aim of their art. Stories have numerous affective benefits for social and emotional development. A story session is a time to share feelings. A relaxed, happy relationship between storyteller and listener is established, drawing them together and building mutual confidence. Stories help children to know themselves and to know others so they can cope with the psychological problems of growing up.

Storytelling brings to the listeners heightened awareness-asense of wonder, of mystery, of reverence for life. Thisnurturing of the spirit-self comes first. It is the primarypurpose of storytelling, and all other uses and effects aresecondary.

Storytelling is also a living art. Like music and dance, it is brought to life in performance. A story will be altered by the storyteller's background: his/her choice of setting and detail, and the rapport established with the audience. The storyteller's building materials are words, sounds, and language patterns. The tools are the voice, face, and hands. The product is the creation of a shared human experience based on words and imagination.

Storytelling is an individual art, and an imposed method or ready-to-use plan will prove inadequate. Beginning storytellers must go beyond the rules. They must know their personal strengths and develop their own unique style. The art of storytelling lies within the storyteller, to be searched for, drawn out, made to grow.

Learning the Story: Steps and Techniques for Teachers and Students

Big Ideas – Start with the big ideas and build your stories around them.

Overheads – Use these to help you and your students tell a story. The illustrations from a story may help you remember the storyline.

Props and/or Costumes – These are not always necessary, but in many cases, simply a hat/cap or artifact may help you tell your story, and may help the listener focus.

Section and Picture – This is a good technique to use to help students retell a story or prepare to tell a story. After reading or listening to a story, ask students to identify the main parts/sections, in sequential order. Divide the class into small groups so that each group has a main part/section to work on. Using butcher/chart paper, ask students to work in their small groups to illustrate those main parts of the story. When done, display illustrations in sequential order and invite a representative(s) from each group to stand before the class to retell the story. While referring to the illustration, encourage students to retell the story from their memory, imagination and collective work with their small group. Let them r know that you are not expecting a "perfect" retelling of the story as they read or heard it.

Storytelling in Groups / Group Storytelling – As with the above activity, offer opportunities to tell stories as a group. Also, invite students to share/tell stories in pairs or small groups to lower anxiety and build skills.

Interactive Storytelling – Look for ways to engage your listeners so they actually become participants in the story. Pattern stories work well since students usually pick up on the repetitive line(s) or story sequence. Solicit their assistance in providing background sounds, standing in as characters, etc.

Storytelling Exercises – Use every opportunity to build your students' skills as storytellers. Even a few minutes each day to play with inflection, body language, facial expression, colorful language, etc. will benefit your storytelling. Students love to talk... let them talk by giving them a purpose, topic, rationale, motivation, etc. Build these kinds of opportunities into your class:

— Sharing

— Talk arounds

— Choral reading

— Dramatic exercises

— Book talks and literature circles

— Socratic seminar

— Capturing stories (use journals or post-its to capture and store those great ideas that pop-up during class)

Storytelling Environment – Build a positive, inviting, conducive environment for storytelling that lowers anxieties and nurtures the development of all storytellers with:

— Exposure to good, plentiful literature

— Integration of social studies, language arts and visual and performing arts

— Opportunities for discussion and constructing meaning of the curriculum

Tell It Your Way – Personalize a story. Make it your own.

SEVEN STEPS TO STORYTELLING

— Select a story you want to tell.

— Learn the structure and block the story.

— Visualize the settings and characters.

— See the action taking place as if you're watching a silent movie.

— Tell the story aloud, using your voice to project the images you've visualized.

— Learn the story by heart, not word for word.

— Practice telling the story until it comes naturally.

SELECTION

Selection requires an ability to evaluate stories and to discriminate between those that meet your learners' needs and those that do not.

1. *Read, read, read.* Although learning stories directly from other storytellers is the traditional method, you will learn most stories from books. Wide reading gives authority to your telling. Read all types of traditional stories and literary fairy tales, modern tales, picture-books, action stories, romances, fantasies, juvenile fiction, nonfiction, and biographies, etc. Read different versions of the same story.

2. *Choose stories you like.* You can only effectively tell the stories that you feel comfortable with and which have meaning for you. Choose stories that you can tell-beginners should tend towards folk tales for their simplicity of structure and language, and shy away from complex literary tales.

3. *Choose stories appropriate for your learners.* Find stories they will like, and that match their age and language

level. Fairy and folk takes, which blend fantasy and reality, and use repetitive language, are good for beginners. Contemporary stories which treat problems of personal identity with more elaborate language are better suited for more advanced learners.

4. *Choose stories with a simple structure.* Look for a single, clearly defined theme, a well-developed sequential plot, a consistent style, standardized characterization (except perhaps for the protagonist), conflict resolution, dramatic appeal, unity, interesting subject matter, and strong emotional content. Avoid stories with long explanations or descriptions, flashbacks, subplots, and other literary devices that break the flow of a story.

5. *Choose stories with positive values.* We prefer to tell stories that implicitly express joy, compassion, humor, resourcefulness, and other positive aspects of human nature. On the other hand, psychologists tell us not to be excessively concerned about violence, fear, anger, hatred, lying, etc., in stories.

6. Study the story's background. Know something of the cultural, social and historical background of the story and the country of its origin. If you can't put the story in context, and its contents are not universal, consider choosing another.

7. Test your selection. Final selection is done through trial, ultimately through the positive or negative reactions you get from your audience.

There are many places to find stories to use, adapt, etc. You may have to look no further than your bookcase, textbook, and newspapers.

— Picture books

— Anthologies

— Collections of myths, legends, fables, folktales
— Autobiographies
— Primary sources
— Textbooks
— Newspaper and magazine articles
— Family stories
— Oral histories and/or personal interviews
— Poetry (in tandem, too!)
— Personal journal entries
— Photo albums
— Videos, films, TV shows, baseball games
— Artifacts to build stories around
— Postcards

USING THE STORY

— Introducing an era, concept, theme, culture, etc.
— Contextualizing information
— Reinforcing, internalizing information
— Integrating the curriculum
— Addressing multiple intelligences and learning styles
— Teaching cultural awareness
— Comparing and contrasting myths, legends, stories
— Identifying and teaching multiple perspectives
— Teaching history through authentic oral tradition
— Bringing history and historical figures to life!

— Exhibitions

— Reward

— Evaluation

— Fun!

Preparation

1. *Learn the story.* Learning the story means to make the story your own. Read it from beginning to end several times. Read it out loud. Master the structure of the story: the beginning (introduction of characters), the body (building of conflict), and the climax (resolution of con- flict). Visualize the succession of scenes. Work on creating sensual setting and character descriptions. Note unusual expressions, word patterns, rhymes, and dialog.
2. *Outline the story.* Storytellers agree that memorizing word for word is not useful. Learn a story incident by incident, and prepare notes that will help you remember this structure. Typed skeleton outlines stick in the minds of visual learners. Cue card outlines are also useful in preparation and storage of tales, but should not be used in telling.
3. *Control the story's length.* Long stories can be simplified or serialized, but not excessively modified or censored. Time yourself during practice. A "story hour" should probably include a mixture of activities: reading storybooks, listening to story tapes, reciting poetry, singing songs, playing games, etc. besides the oral story itself.
4. *Control the story's vocabulary.* A rich vocabulary, with carefully chosen adjectives and adverbs, gives color and texture to the telling. However, you need to be

comfortable with your use of language and not try too hard to get things "right" or the story will come out flat and nervous. Don't worry if the listeners don't already know every word; guessing is part of language learning.

5. *Refine your storytelling style.* Tell the story aloud to listen to your voice - your instrument - which you can exercise, train, and even change. A pause and dropped voice are often more effective than shouting. Take poetic passages slowly; report conversation at natural speed; tell narration more rapidly, building toward the climax.

6. *Practice, practice, practice.* Practice aloud to yourself, your family or friends. You could practice on audio or even video tape. Practice in front of a mirror to eliminate poor gestures and facial expressions. Some say practice makes storytelling artificial and studied, but it is essential to the beginner.

7. *Relax before telling.* Warm up as the situation allows with breathing, stretching, and vocal exercises.

PRESENTATION

A story should be presented in a way that emphasizes the "what" of the story and not the "how" of the telling.

1. *Start on the right foot.* The beginning introduces the characters, sets the scene, establishes the mood, defines the conflict or predicament of the protagonist, and arouses pleasurable anticipation. Then the narrative carries the action. It is sometimes essential for comprehension, before beginning a tale, to make some background comments on new or difficult vocabulary or the cultural assumptions and setting of the story. You might share an object related to the story or light

a ritual candle to signal the beginning of the special storytelling time.

2. *Be your best self.* Express enthusiasm, spontaneity, creativity, and enjoyment. You can create a mood through your physical appearance and mannerisms. Don't rush or ramble. Don't be condescending or phony. Don't reveal nervousness or embarrassment. And most of all, don't let your technique show.
3. *Concentrate on your voice.* The audience absolutely must hear everything loudly and clearly! Try for a pleasant, intimate, smooth, low-pitched tone of voice. You will need vocal energy for projection, articulation, enunciation, and intonation. Altering your speed and pitch-for example, giving different tones to different characters-adds to the emotional impact.
4. *Maintain eye contact.* Eye contact is of the utmost importance as it not only holds the listener's attention and involves the listener in the story, but it checks understanding and gives instant feedback.
5. *Help with your hands and body.* The hands also create. Use only gestures that come naturally, but be aware of your hands; don't hide them or flap them about. Facial expressions and movement are also vital aids. Some tellers use very limited movement; others almost mime a story.
6. *Use props sparingly.* Some storytellers are strongly against the use of any objects, puppets, costumes, bells, etc. They consider them a clever showman's device and an unnecessary distraction.
7. *Pay attention to the physical setting.* Some rooms can kill a good story. You need a quiet, well-lit, acoustically acceptable, comfortable space. You can tell a story standing up (for more freedom of movement)

or sitting on a stool (for better eye-contact) before a semi-circle of chairs or (for more intimacy) sitting in a tight circle on a carpet.

Follow-Up Activities

While no follow-up is necessary-stories are valuable in their own right, but a variety of options are available.

1. *Ask comprehension questions carefully.* If a story is followed immediately by a barrage of comprehension questions, its artistic value is lost and storytelling suffers. I would suggest waiting at least a day to ask the usual who, what, where, when, how much, and why questions. There are other, more creative ways to use questions. Multiple choice questions and questions that can be answered by inference can be used. Suppositions can be made, like: What would you have done? What should the character have done? Students may choose from a list of questions provided by the teacher and ask a partner. It's even possible to give out comprehension questions first and have the students construct the story.

2. *Invent exercises in phonetics, semantics, and syntax.* There is no limit to the language exercises that can be based on a story: introduction of new vocabulary in lexical sets, rhyming sets, or grammatical sets; verbal practice and grammatical analysis of repeated phrases: "Who's been sleeping in my bed?" "I'll huff, and I'll puff and I'll blow the house down," just to name a few.

3. *Do listening activities.* After a tale, listeners can demonstrate comprehension by: comparing, discriminating, predicting, sequencing, classifying, transferring information, etc. Unlike other listening activities, stories are often repeated, but never in exactly the same words.

4. *Do oral activities.* Choral reading, story fill-in, add-on stories, building a tale from key words, etc., are all options. Discussion topics can be taken from the story's themes. Students can retell their favorite tales, or invent stories based on their own personal experiences.

5. *Do written activities.* Rewriting, summarizing, or paraphrasing a tale are obvious and worthwhile activities. Written exercises can include controlled writing dictation and cloze paragraphs, guided writing (sentence extension or sentence-combining exercises), or free writing using the tale as a literary model. Other options include: journal writing, research projects, making up original stories patterned on stories told to the group, and writing a poem or a play version of a story.

6. *Do visual activities.* Story-related artwork can include: posters, models, collages, crafts, masks, puppets, mobiles, photos, picture stories, blackboard drawing, etc. Stories are part of aesthetic education and develop creativity.

7. *Do creative drama activities.* There are many story games to play. Stories naturally lend themselves to be dramatized, mimed, or roleplayed. Prepared dialogs from tales can be recited, or students can tell or retell stories they choose or make up themselves.

Stories educate, illustrate, enlighten, and inspire. They give relief from the routine and stimulate the mind. They are a great motivator for teachers as well as for students. Stories are used in an exclusively positive scholastic setting, i.e., no grades, no failures, no textbooks, no notepads, no dictionaries, no costly audiovisual equipment- nothing coming between the listener and the teller. In EFL, stories fosternderstanding and acceptance of the foreign language and culture.

Storytelling is learned slowly over a long time, but the novice and the expert storyteller can both experience success on different levels. A storyteller eventually makes a personal collection of stories for various occasions and purposes. Storytelling is a folk-art which can't be manipulated, intellectualized, or mass-produced. Its magic is unique. The storyteller is always a teacher, and the teacher is always a storyteller.

Power of Storytelling

Storytelling is one of the oldest, if not *the* oldest method of communicating ideas and images. Story performance honed our mythologies long before they were written and edited by scribes, poets, or scholars. Storytelling, as it is defined here, is a linguistic activity that is educative because it allows individuals to share their personal understanding with others, thereby creating negotiated transactions.Without this interactive narrative experience humans could not express their knowledge or thought. As Bruner points out, storytelling is part of how humans translate their individual private experience of understanding into a public culturally negotiated form. Storytelling is also a performance art, one that has been revitalized in recent years and which has developed into a neotradition throughout the U.S.A.

Today, the modern storyteller performs texts that (for most) have been learned from books. However, the art of storytelling still remains connected to its ancient roots in that it remains an activity where a tale is told aloud, to an audience, without the use of memorized scripts or other literary texts. It is the closest thing we have, in modern contexts, to the orality of our preliterate ancestors. Modern storytellers, therefore, like their ancient counterparts, continue to rely on their manipulation of language in order to relate an anecdote and often make use of dramatic skills such as characterization, narration, vocalization, and mimetic action.

Traditional texts have been passed on through storytelling across the generations, developed by way of the folk process, and resulting in archetypal culturally shared narratives that have educative value. Literary forms of these tales, as we know them today, were originally collected, transcribed, edited, published, and subsequently used as source material for much of the current literature for children as well as the fantasy fiction for adults. Still, due to the fact that many tellers crafted myths and legends in a variety of social contexts, over time, these stories remain illustrative of collective experiences. Many traditional texts define ethical perspectives, epistemological views, and cultural constructions of identities and it is generally thought that the folk process strengthened the collective or social knowledge, contained in stories. The evolution of folk tales, then, evolved into primary texts for learning and meaning making.

The concept, that stories characterize and define identity, for both individuals and groups, is also grounded in the work of Jung who identifies a series of specific and formal elements within world mythologies that have become primary archetypes. Each archetype represents a core psychological function common to all humans. Jung's archetypes are found symbolically within traditional tales and are depicted in a variety of forms. The fact that many of these archetypes occur repetitively in myths from widely divergent geographical areas is evidence, according to Jung, that a "collective unconscious" exists connecting people, cultures, and time within a "generative force."

Bettelheim, a Freudian psychoanalyst, has also argued that stories are symbolic expressions of the inner experience of development in children. Stories connect children to psychological realities and folk tales assist children in their psychosocial and imaginative growth. When traditional texts are told to children, according to Bettelheim, the symbolic patterns these tales display become manifestations of psychological constructs.

The work of Bettelheim and Jung profoundly influenced the field of education. Developmental models extracted from traditional literatures by these theorists suggested to many educators, at the time, that stories were important teaching tools and that children would benefit from exposure folk tales. Applebee and Favat, in their originative studies, examined children's reactions to folk stories and found that students made connections between the plots and events in books by connecting their own life experiences to that of fictional characters. This research encouraged more educators to take stories seriously and to incorporate them in teaching and learning environments.

Wells's seminal study investigating the links between storytelling and school success found that the key to literacy development was consistent exposure to storytelling and narrative discourse in both the home and classroom environments. Wells' work has strengthened efforts to incorporate storytelling in school environments. Current studies support Well's findings, suggesting that telling stories from culturally diverse sources supports the creation of multicultural awareness in classrooms and encourages the development of healthy self-concepts.

Traditional literatures from a wide variety of cultural contexts have also been found useful in the growth of imagination, morality and self-identity. In addition, Egan suggests that the dramatic format of Western story itself can function within classrooms as the primary form of teaching and learning. In addition, he finds that "the classic fairy tales have considerable power to engage the imaginations of young children in classroom settings".

Although storytelling is now maturing into a recognized performance-art form, as indicated by the current popularity of storytellers' guilds, artist-residency programs, university courses, publications, and international conferences, it still takes a back seat to other more technological forms of instruction. In spite of the fact that storytelling as teaching has the strongest support in preschool and kindergarten classrooms-where it is an important accepted method of teaching-it is still not a common and consistent practice across grades and content areas.

Because children are currently the major consumers of traditional texts in our society, the question of how folk tales may or may not impact learning remains important to our understanding of education and human development. However, few studies exist that actually investigate the impact of the ancient and seminal performing art of storytelling on children's development and learning.

The simple reason why storytelling is becoming a major factor in management and organizations is that it works. Purposeful storytelling can get results in the modern organization that traditional abstract modes of communications can't.

— *An old technology with a modern use.* It draws on aspects of human nature of which we are barely aware and makes use of a delivery system that is as old as civilization itself – the spare evocative story – storytelling recovers a technique for inviting people into the process of change.

— *A powerful technology:* Purposeful storytelling can reach large numbers of people amazingly rapidly. People get the idea, not slowly and painfully by the accumulation of evidence and meticulous elaboration of multiple dimensions. With storytelling, people can get the idea in a flash.

— *Getting results now*: Purposeful storytelling is a tool for getting thing done in the world, getting business results. Storytelling delivers. Because it delivers so quickly, it is in tune with the web-speed economy.

— *The technology is free:* Storytelling doesn't require expensive investments in hardware or software. It doesn't involve recruiting expensive experts. Storytelling is the ultimate low-cost high-return technology.

— *Everyone already a storyteller:* We start learning to tell stories and listen to stories at the age of two, and spend the rest of our lives telling stories. Storytelling is so pervasive that we are as unconscious of it as we are of the air we breathe. It is something we know already how to do.

— *Everyone can be a better storyteller:* Though we all tell stories all the time, we are often unaware of it. Once we realize what are doing, we can all learn not only to become better storytellers but also to use storytelling to business results.

— *Everyone can get results from storytelling:* The understanding of storytelling and the development of technique enables one to use get organization and management results from storytelling. It's the purposeful telling of stories, not accidental narrative.

— *We need to unlearn what we have been (mis)-taught.* We start out life as storytellers, and then we are taught at school to unlearn this technology, to use abstract language. We are taught that knowledge is abstract and storytelling is for children. In our private lives, we ignore the advice. But the same technology can also be used at work. We need to realize that stories not only function socially but can be used for serious purposes to get results fast.

11

Teaching of Spelling

Most pupils regularly carry out pre-writing activities in nursery and reception, such as forming letter shapes in sand, over-writing and underwriting. Most also receive a good grounding in basic phonic work as they move through the reception year and into the start of key stage 1. They learn initial sounds, common digraphs, initial consonant clusters and simple endings. Many schools also emphasise effective listening skills—for example 'stretching' out words to hear their component parts and breaking words down into segments or words within words. They also stress the building of a spelling vocabulary of high-frequency words which can be recognised by sight and sound.

The teaching of regular sound-symbol relationships is the focus of much key stage 1 teaching. At the end of key stage 1, and as pupils move through key stage 2, pupils are beginning to understand that sound-letter relationships are sometimes quite complex and that if they rely only on a narrow set of such rules or relationships, they will make many spelling errors. This is especially true of pupils in Welsh-medium schools who move at the start of key stage 2 from a consistent sound-letter relationship in Welsh to a more diverse system in English.

Good spellers are able to broaden their knowledge and understanding of spelling as they move through the school. They learn that the sound of a word is only one guide to its spelling and they use their knowledge of exceptions, simple and complex rules and their visual memory to help them master spelling. Better spellers also often have an interest in words for their own sake and they are keen to think about aspects of the form and structure of words, root words, prefixes and suffixes, loan words and word derivations.

Problems occur for many pupils as they move through key stage 1 and begin to meet the demands of the key stage 2 curriculum. In key stage 1, many pupils struggle to spell words with:

— more than one syllable where the relationship between the sound and letter is not straightforward;

— double consonants, especially at the end of words; and

— vowel digraphs such as 'gh', especially in the middle of words.

In key stage 2, the same difficulties as in key stage 1 often remain, and other difficulties begin to appear. At this point, pupils commonly make the following types of mistakes:

— they struggle with vowel digraphs, especially representing the long 'e' sound;

— they are unsure about doubling of consonants in the middle of words or before '-ed' and '-ly' endings;

— they misspell unstressed syllables and more complex clusters of consonants;

— they omit letters, especially when trying to form the past tense (as in 'happend') or they leave out a final 'e';

— they join separate words together (as in 'aswell');

— they add inappropriate hyphens (as in 'today'); and

— they divide up words inappropriately (as in 'some one', 'with out' and 'where ever').

The problems for weak spellers in key stage 2 also relate to the increasing language demands of the curriculum. It is very common for problems with spelling in key stages 1 and 2 to continue through into work in key stages 3 and 4. As pupils move from key stage to key stage, the challenge in relation to spelling increases as:

— words and sentences become longer and more varied;

— the range of specialist vocabulary increases;

— writing demands become more diverse; and

— children meet more exceptions to previously learnt 'rules'.

Weak spellers often attempt to spell unfamiliar words by using a simple sound-letter strategy or by drawing on their memory of similar sounding words. In many instances, it is easy to see why the pupil spells the word in that way—even though it is wrong. The spelling mistake comes from making good use of previous knowledge.

However, when a pupil makes spelling mistakes with a word that has been met many times before, then there is clearly an underlying problem with the learning. The pupil can be stuck in a narrow set of simple sound-letter relationships or may lack a range of strategies to check the accuracy of their spellings. In these cases pupils are unable to lock new spellings into their minds.

Teachers encourage pupils to sound out or 'stretch' a word to help them hear all the sounds within it. Teachers often exaggerate the sounds to make the pupils aware of what their lips, tongue, teeth and breath are doing to produce them. Breaking a word down into units of sound often has a positive effect on the pupils' ability to spell a word, especially where the teacher focuses on the likely spelling of each constituent sound.

Teachers often use rhyme to emphasise and reinforce particular sounds and combinations of letters. A strong emphasis on rhyme delivers an important message to pupils about the relationship between a sound and the way it is written. Sharing a rhyming poem in class also helps pupils to produce more words of their own, with the same sound and written form.

Teachers introduce a class book and focus on a high frequency word in the text. They encourage pupils to recognise the word throughout the text. They point out any aspects of the word that are interesting and which may help the pupils to develop an understanding of it and other words like it. They use the white board and coloured magnetic letters to focus pupils' attention on the letters in the word.

The teacher encourages pupils to come forward and make new words based on the chosen word. The teacher asks pupils to change the initial or final letter. The teacher chooses the high frequency word carefully according to a plan agreed by all the staff. The words become more complex as the pupils move through the school. By the end of key stage 2, the shared text may be an information text in science or an extract from a Shakespearean play.

Teachers help pupils to understand the way certain words are spelt by making pupils aware of the words within other longer words. Pupils often use this knowledge to fix certain useful spellings in their minds. For example, they see 'break' and 'fast' in 'breakfast', 'cup' and 'board' in 'cupboard' and 'a rat' in 'separate'. This approach helps pupils even when the constituent syllables do not all form separate words, as in 'Wednesday', but the focus on small units of spelling helps pupils to spell the longer word.

Teachers introduce letters and sounds in a clearly structured way following an order agreed by all staff in the school. For example, reception teachers are aware that they need to introduce initial sounds first, then final sounds, as well as some basic consonant digraphs, perhaps 'ch', 'sh' and 'th', and a set of simple consonant-vowelconsonant words. All staff agree the order in which they will teach these aspects.

When words arise that are exceptions to common spelling patterns, effective teachers do not make much of them in the early stages for fear of confusing pupils who are at the stage of making patterns and connections in their minds. In the early stages, teachers keep the focus on the written forms they have introduced. Teachers often make effective judgements about the words that pupils suggest in class discussion in terms of how useful they are in reinforcing the spelling patterns they are currently teaching. Teachers make these sensitive decisions far more regularly as pupils move through infants and into juniors.

Effective teachers introduce spelling patterns in a way that fits pupils' development as writers and in relation to the frequency with which they are likely to come across the pattern in their own reading and writing.

Effective teachers of spelling give pupils knowledge of the spelling system as well as an ability to spell words correctly. With this knowledge, pupils are far more able to make sensible choices when spelling unfamiliar words. For example, a Year 2 pupil might write 'bred' instead of 'bread' when writing about food. 'Bred' is a sensible spelling choice. However, the pupil still needs to be encouraged to think of another way to write the word ('bread') and then to look at both choices and see which one looks right.

If that is not enough then the pupil may need to check the word in a dictionary before finally deciding on the right choice. However, a teacher of pupils in a reception class might praise the pupil's use of 'bred' for 'bread', if they have only introduced the 'e' grapheme for the sound at that stage. On balance, this does not hamper the development of accurate spelling so long as there is a clearly understood strategy for moving forward as pupils learn more and more letter-sound relationships.

Effective teachers know that some words have a spelling which is so different from the normal pattern that pupils will have to memorise them if they are to spell them accurately in their own writing. Many of these words are important and appear often in pupils' reading and writing and most pupils do not have a problem learning them by sight.

Most teachers also use 'Look Cover Write Check' as an effective method to teach pupils both how to try out a spelling first where they are unsure about it and as a way of fixing the spelling of words into pupils' visual memory. Many teachers use this technique effectively as an activity following their marking of pupils' writing.

Effective teachers of spelling know that some basic spelling rules can provide pupils with the help they need to spell many words correctly. A basic rule, such as 'q is always followed by a u', can help even very weak spellers. Most rules rely on an understanding of the basic features of letters and words, such as consonant, vowel, short vowel, past tense, suffix and prefix. Effective teachers introduce rules appropriately and sensitively when pupils know these ideas and terms well.

Once pupils have developed a reasonable degree of confidence in reading, then comparing words such as 'hoping' and 'hopping' can provide a useful basis to discuss the effect of one consonant compared to two on the length of the vowel sound. In the best instances, teachers actively encourage pupils to investigate words in this way and to speculate about the rules that lie behind the way we spell words. Researching the plurals of words with 'y' endings, such as 'baby'/'babies' and 'journey'/'journeys', can stimulate pupils' interest in the spelling system and lock spellings and various spelling patterns and rules into their minds successfully. Work on prefixes and suffixes can also produce useful strategies for pupils to use in their spelling, for example in looking at words like 'unnecessary' or 'sincerely'.

In a classroom where there is effective teaching of spelling, teachers often:

— use displays of word charts to encourage pupils to check for spellings;

— use 'Look, Cover, Write, Check' or 'Have a go' books for pupils to practise and to see if their spelling of a word looks right;

— use a white-board to demonstrate words, digraphs, words within words, high-frequency words;

— display 'problem' words on a classroom word bank;

— use commercially-produced material effectively, such as phoneme/grapheme charts or phonic flash cards; and. use various software packages to teach spelling in short bursts.

Welsh-medium Schools Teaching Spelling

The relationship between sounds and letters is generally far more consistent in Welsh than in English. This means that pupils in Welsh-medium schools, many of whom have been successful in learning Welsh spelling patterns, may face particular challenges in learning the English spelling system. In some Welsh-medium schools, pupils start to read and write in English during the last term of Year 2. In these and in all other Welsh-medium schools, Year 3 is crucially important in the development of pupils' spelling in English.

Good teaching of spelling is the same whether it is in the Welsh or English language and has many of the characteristics already mentioned. However, effective teachers at the start of Year 3 know that there are some common spelling errors which happen because pupils apply rules which they have learned in Welsh to their new language, namely English. Effective teachers of English spelling in Welsh-medium schools use the following strategies:

— they focus on letters which sound similar in English and Welsh, but which are spelt differently, for example 'th' (as in 'the') and 'dd' (as in ddiwrnod), 'f' (as in 'feet') and 'ff' (as in 'ffrind');

— they introduce patterns and rhymes in English spelling and compare these to the Welsh spelling of words which also seem to rhyme, for example, 'hide', 'side', 'ride', 'tide' in English and 'paid', 'rhaid', 'taid' in Welsh;

— they introduce pupils to words for the same thing which are different in North and South Wales, for example 'llaeth/llefrith', 'gwdihw/tylluan', 'gyda/efo' and 'merch/hogan', to alert pupils to look for differences and similarities in language from an early age and to help them tune into differences between completely different languages, like Welsh and English;

— they are alert to the potential for interference between pupils' English and Welsh spelling in the later years of key stage 2, when pupils have become much more competent spellers in English, and teachers continue to focus on the differences between the two languages, for example, 'I'd' in English and 'i'r' in Welsh where many pupils use the capital 'I' in both languages; and. they encourage pupils in key stage 2 to use their knowledge of Welsh to find the meaning of English words and to learn to spell them correctly, for example 'tripartite' and 'mellifluous'.

SCHOOLS PLAN FOR EFFECTIVE SPELLING

In the best instances, schools have a plan that sets out the expectations for the teacher and the pupils from early years through to Year 6. Where there are separate infant and junior schools, staff work hard to agree a common strategy across the two schools for the benefit of the pupils. In Welsh-medium schools, as outlined above, teachers plan the introduction of features of English spelling very carefully and take advantage of pupils' knowledge and understanding of Welsh spelling.

Effective schools set out a route map for pupils' spelling. This usually takes the form of a plan for each year group that identifies for the teacher what elements of the spelling programme they are to cover. In many schools, the plan is further broken down into terms. Where planning for spelling is sound, there are clear joins between long-term plans (what pupils should learn over the year), midterm plans (what pupils should learn over the term) and the teacher's short-term planning (what pupils should learn over the week).

Pupils make better progress in spelling where they receive the same messages about spelling from class to class as they grow older. Where there is a clear plan and where staff have agreed a whole-school approach, teachers are able to make good use of what pupils have learned previously. Pupils also receive positive messages about the overall coherence of the spelling system itself when they receive consistent messages about it. It hampers pupils' progress where teachers introduce aspects of spelling before pupils have the relevant knowledge or understanding or where they teach aspects which have already been covered in some depth. Where teachers plan in isolation from each other, pupils often do not make the best possible progress.

Many schools plan carefully the introduction of various high frequency words that pupils learn by sight. Many of these words have irregular or difficult spellings and pupils need to become familiar with their spelling at an early stage if their writing is to progress well. In effective schools, teachers are very aware of these words, display them well in the classroom and focus upon them regularly in pupils' reading and writing, especially throughout key stage 1.

Pupils make the best progress where spelling is an integral part of their writing for a real purpose. Most schools begin by teaching aspects of spelling one at a time and build up pupils' knowledge of spelling as time progresses. However, in the best instances, pupils use their developing knowledge of spelling in regular writing tasks which have a real purpose and audience. Pupils may spend some time completing written exercises which focus on a specific aspect of spelling, but staff know that the final aim is for the pupils to use their spelling knowledge in their own writing.

On occasions, some schools do not get the balance right and place too much emphasis on pupils completing written exercises which are not linked to real purposes and audiences. In these instances, pupils often complete the spelling exercises correctly, and sometimes achieve full marks, but their spelling in real writing tasks shows that they have not really learnt how to spell correctly.

Some schools teach spelling as a part of a wider published scheme that often focuses on the systematic development of pupils' knowledge of phonics. Many of these schemes work well because they establish a clear framework for pupils' learning and develop pupils' knowledge of sounds and letters in a coherent way. Where schools adopt such schemes and deliver them effectively:

— the whole school discusses the merits of the approach;

— the headteacher and staff agree a common way forward;

— the subject leader adapts the existing policy and planning documents to take account of the new approaches;

— teachers undertake training to deliver the scheme;

— the staff establish a set of criteria they will use to judge whether the new scheme has been a success or not; and

— the headteacher and subject co-ordinator monitor the effectiveness of the new scheme and report back regularly to staff and the governing body on progress, especially the outcomes in terms of spelling ages and results in national tests.

However, the best schools know that these schemes need to be supplemented by other methods to make sure that the pupils develop spelling strategies which do not rely solely on the relationship between sounds and letters.

Effective schools know that parents can make an important impact on supporting pupils' learning. Schools inform parents how their children learn about spelling and some of the strategies teachers use. They also inform parents about ways in which they can support the school's efforts to improve pupils' spelling, for example by stressing the 'Look Cover Write Check' approach when their child is writing at home. Parents are also told about the 'sounding out' technique and breaking words down into units where these strategies might be helpful. Parents of young children can place simple word cards on objects or furniture about the home and can encourage older children to use a dictionary.

Where the planning is effective, teachers are very aware of the types of spelling errors that occur in pupils' writing at different stages of their development as writers. Teachers know the words likely to cause the most problems with each year group and across the ability range. Good schools have effective plans to deal with spelling errors that occur time and time again in pupils' writing. Some teachers plan short sessions for the whole class to revise a certain aspect. Others take a small group of children who share the same problem and focus on improving their spelling in that area with some additional exercises to reinforce the learning.

Schools Analyse Pupile's Spelling

Effective schools have a marking policy that all staff agree with and follow. The best policies offer a balance between support and encouragement to the pupil and the need to identify errors to aid pupils' learning and to eliminate errors in the future.

Effective teachers mark pupils' spelling in a way that fits the pupils' stage of development as a writer and speller. It is common for teachers in the reception class and in the early part of key stage 1 to mark only those errors which show that the pupil is struggling with a particular aspect or which is the focus of the work. For example, when a teacher of pupils in the reception class sees a pupil writing 'sed' instead of 'said', the response may be a positive one when the teacher has just introduced the words 'red' and 'bed'. However, once the teacher has introduced the word 'said', the teacher's response to 'sed' will be different and the error may be marked and noted.

Teachers spend a lot of time marking pupils' work and much of it is spent identifying spelling errors. Marking is effective when teachers give some thought to the focus of the marking. On many occasions, spelling may not be the chief focus. However, effective marking of a spelling error should mean that the pupil responds to it. In effective schools, this usually means that pupils transfer the word to a spelling book or to a list of words at the back of their writing books or at the end of the piece of writing itself. Pupils frequently use the 'Look Cover Write Check' approach to lock the correct spelling more firmly into their minds. In the best practice, teachers devise spelling tests for individual pupils that draw from these lists of words.

More and more schools use spelling partners to help pupils support each other's spelling development. In these instances, pupils of similar ability read out words taken from the other pupils' misspellings and key words chosen by the teacher and each one tests the other. Pupils then transfer the results of the paired testing to a simple grid which informs the teacher of the pupils' progress. In effective schools this is a powerful learning tool and adds relevance to the teacher's marking of spelling in pupils' written work.

In effective schools, especially in key stage 2, spelling is one element within an overall approach to drafting and editing pupils' written work. In the best practice, pupils focus on the content, structure and organisation of the writing and spell as accurately as they can first time. Pupils then edit their work and check the accuracy of their spelling. In the worst examples, pupils focus too much on spelling at the first draft stage. They spend too long waiting for the teacher to check a word or they consult a dictionary for almost every other word. In these instances, pupils often make very slow progress and write relatively little.

Most teachers, especially in key stage 1, encourage pupils to build up their own word books where they can try out the spelling of words they are worried about and which they need for their writing. In the best practice, the pupil will always 'have a go' and try to spell the word first. In many cases they are correct, the teacher encourages the pupil and gradually their confidence grows. On those occasions when they 'have a go' and the spelling is wrong, the teacher can help the pupil by looking for patterns in the word to remember, sounding it out where this is helpful or underlining a part of the word to focus the pupil's attention on the incorrect element.

Often these prompts are enough for the pupil to get the word right and the teacher is showing the pupil techniques that they can try for themselves in the future. The teacher only writes the word for the pupil after the pupil has tried to bring their previous knowledge and understanding to bear on the word. In the best practice, pupils learn this approach themselves and help each other when problems arise. In the worst practice, the teacher immediately writes the word for the pupil. This often leads to pupils relying too much on the teacher for many of their words.

Many schools analyse the spelling of pupils in the National Curriculum (NC) tests and tasks and use the results to draw conclusions about the effectiveness of the school's teaching of spelling. Using this approach, schools have begun to set specific targets for spelling, for example, to reduce the proportion of errors in the spelling component of the NC tests from 50% to 15%. Other schools have looked at patterns of errors in the writing component of the tests and have used the information to plan work on specific aspects.

Many pupils who achieve Level 2C in the NC test for writing are weak spellers. Many of these pupils rely very heavily on basic phonic knowledge for their spelling choices and have a weak sight vocabulary. As a result of this, a number of schools have increased their emphasis on high frequency words taught by sight recognition and have begun to use their own checklists of words and spelling patterns as a way of gauging pupils' progress effectively from one year to the next.

Many schools send home lists of words for pupils to learn and then test these spellings in class a few days later. Especially in key stage 1, the words in the list often follow the same spelling pattern. However, pupils' success in these tests is often linked more to their ability to revise and check the words before the test than to their ability as spellers. It is not unusual for some pupils to achieve high scores in these spelling tests, but to misspell many of the same words in their own writing.

Schools Plan of Improve Pupil's Spelling

Schools need to make sure they:

— plan spelling carefully so that each teacher knows what elements of the spelling system they are responsible for teaching in their class;

— help pupils to sound out words and hear the constituent sounds within them;

— make pupils aware of the spelling choices available to them when they need to spell a word;

— develop pupils' ability to 'have a go' at spelling before asking for help or consulting a dictionary;

— make sure pupils develop a good sight vocabulary, especially of high-frequency words with spellings that do not conform to familiar patterns;

— encourage pupils to research and analyse words and spelling patterns;

— make sure teachers' marking of spelling leads to a response from the pupil and improvements in their spelling;

— share with parents the school's approach to teaching spelling so parents can help support the development of their children's spelling at home; and. judge the success of the school's approach to spelling by regularly monitoring and evaluating samples of pupils' writing drawn from across the school.

12

Correcting Errors in English Usage

There are two main reasons are appealing for research to help local ESL (English as a Second Language) teachers deliver sound, effective error-correction feedback in class. The first reason is that there is an obvious need for it. As is well-known, the written English output of both secondary and tertiary students in Hong Kong tends to be fraught with proficiency problems. Many teachers of English are under great pressure, especially from school principals and panel chairs, to correct student errors, with the tacit assumption that the correction will be noticed by the learner and subsequently make a difference in the learner's ESL competence. There is, however, substantial empirical research evidence showing that this assumption is not always warranted.

Subject-verb agreement is one notorious example. Despite it having been pointed out by their teachers through error-correction feedback, many ESL learners continue to have this problem in free writing. While recognise that not all errors can be removed through the teacher's correction, together with clear pedagogical information and instructions for the ESL teacher as to how these errors can be effectively corrected, has a good potential for helping learners self-monitor, cope with and eventually overcome at least some persistent errors more efficiently and effectively.

The second reason has to do with renewed interests in error analysis in Second Language Acquisition (SLA) research. The two paradigms in SLA research: contrastive analysis (CA) and error analysis (EA), which were much discredited during the 1970s and early 1980s have recently been revitalised following significant works in the past decade, notably by James, 1998; Kellerman; Kellerman & Sharwood-Smith; Odlin.

Many of the basic premises of CA, be it the strong or the weak version, have been refined, with its focus and purpose shifted from predicting learner difficulties and errors to accounting for the complex processes of transfer, which may be positive or negative depending on the outcome of learning. The shift in emphasis has given rise to a new name for the paradigm: crosslinguistic influence. EA, being a post-hoc analytical instrument with all its methodological limitations, remains a useful means to uncover some of the cognitive, linguistic, and pragmatic complexities involved in SLA.

Since it is well-known that structural comparisons of two languages are uncertain correlates of learner behaviour", at least in the Hong Kong language situation, establishing an empirically based taxonomy of typical learner errors is somehow one preliminary and crucial step towards a better understanding of the cognitive and psycholinguistic mechanisms at work in the ESL learning process.

Without an understanding of such mechanisms, teachers may not be aware of the 'gravity' of learner errors and therefore will be ill-advised or unsure as to how best to help their students improve their language accuracy. At the same time, reliable information about typical structural and vocabulary learning problems at different proficiency levels can stimulate ESL researchers, syllabus designers and curriculum writers to anticipate learning problems, focus their remedial efforts, and to try out error-correction activities and consolidating exercises.

Though there exist quite a few local publications on the common ESL errors of local students, they contain little or no pedagogically viable information on effective error correction for teacher-users. There is thus a need for local ESL researchers to:

— identify salient error types commonly found among Hong Kong Chinese students with a view to establishing a taxonomy of common structural and lexical errors at three more or less discrete proficiency levels: elementary, intermediate and advanced;

— delimit a subset of high-frequency errors and explore pedagogically sound methods and techniques to overcome them; and

— design and experiment with error-correction instructions and activities to help teachers and learners overcome those ESL learning difficulties identified.

To help local ESL teachers deliver pedagogically sound and viable error-correction feedback, data-driven taxonomy based on well-defined, high-frequency structural and lexical errors is a necessary prerequisite.

Areas of Focus

It is well-known that errors are indicative of the learners' interlanguage, representing systematic deviations from the norms of the target language in the language learning process. When the error is wholly attributable to the learner's mother tongue, it is said to be the result of L1 interference, hence 'interlingual' error. On the other hand, if the error may be shown to be caused by problems acquiring the target language itself, it is usually considered as a developmental, or 'intralingual' error. More often than not, however, the errors made along the learner's interlanguage continuum are due to a complex interplay between both L1- and L2-related factors.

While the identification of the source(s) and cause(s) of an error may or may not be of much help in ridding the anomaly in question, establishing two complementary taxonomies-a taxonomy of structural errors supported by a taxonomy of lexical errors-has a greater potential for helping target users appreciate how the error may be overcome.

Teachability

The higher the degree of teachability of a given error type, the easier it would be to formulate and proceduralise pedagogically sound error-correction instruction to overcome that error, and vice versa. Postulate that a given error type may be situated along a teachability continuum, with lexical and structural errors being more amenable to correction, whereas 'hard-core' grammatical errors such as misuse of tenses and articles are less likely to be quickly corrected without the ESL teacher giving detailed explanations supported by contextualised exemplification.

It is not at all straightforward, for example, how ESL learners whose interlanguage generates erroneous sentences such as He is teacher may be enlightened on the correct and proper use of the indefinite article 'a' or 'an'. Likewise, the proper use of tenses in English such as the subtle distinction between present perfect and simple past is not easy to grasp or explain.

As for the choice between written and spoken English data, the former is clearly more manageable, establishing a corpus of written English errors commonly found among local ESL learners of three more or less discrete proficiency levels will be a reasonably feasible intermediate goal. The insights thus derived, may subsequently inform and sharpen up the focus of the target interlanguage structures and lexis in speech.

Structural Anomalies

There has been a fair amount of published research on Hong Kong-specific learner errors. However, compared with the availability of numerous handbooks on common errors intended largely for 'popular consumption', empirical research on errors made by Chinese ESL learners and pedagogically oriented error-correction materials are scanty. Yip is one notable exception.

Drawing on insights from both Universal Grammar and language typology, Yip is a systematic study of Chinese interlanguage (GIL)---a relatively stable grammar which has its own properties and internal logic but which falls short of target language norms. The study is based on mainly production data-written compositions, oral reports, casual conversations-of 20 Chinese ESL learners mostly from Taiwan, who were typically recent arrivals in the United States. Grammaticality judgement questionnaires were also used to tap into the grammatical competence of the learners' interlanguage. Four CIL structures were studied in detail:

— 'pseudo-passives'

— 'ergative constructions'

— 'pseudo-tough movement' and

— 'existential pseudo-relatives'.

While pseudo-passives and existential pseudo-relatives refer to faulty constructions which are more appropriately expressed using a passive and relative structure respectively, sentences with pseudo-tough movement as refer to constructions which cannot be expressed using the tough-movement structure such as English is difficult to learn. Ergative constructions, on the other hand, involve the inappropriate passivisation of ergative verbs which can be used both transitively and intransitively, including the passivisation of verbs which should only be used intransitively.

Among the key findings in Yip are the observations that both transfer from L1 and universal developmental features in language acquisition are attested, and that the degree of learnability of a target language hinges on and may be explained by systematic structural contrasts between L1 and L2.

The comparative lack of research in SLA involving Chinese learners is all the more marked given the fact that native speakers of Chinese make up the largest group of ESL learners today. There is thus a need to investigate systematically how Chinese learners acquire English, what difficulties they encounter, and what errors they make at different stages of the learning process. In addition to the practical objective of helping ESL-teachers deliver quality error-correction feedback, it is believed that research on Hong Kong-specific CIL will inform SLA theories by filling some information gaps that involve the acquisition of English by learners from a typologically distant L1 background such as Cantonese.

Misuse of Words

Apart from rule-governed structural anomalies, many of the accuracy problems may be explained by substandard mastery of content words, especially verbs, nouns and adjectives, in that order. Research in the past two decades has shown that second language vocabulary plays a much more important role than was previously thought to be the case, and therefore should not be disregarded.

In particular, research has shown that accuracy of language use may be significantly improved with the mastery of the correct usage of the vocabulary item. It is in this sense that Gairns & Redman speak of the 'grammar of vocabulary'. Typical examples include the misuse of verb transitivity or confusion between noun and verb forms, preposition, or plural form of an uncountable noun. This insight helps justify why for local ESL teachers, curriculum writers and syllabus designers, a separate, pedagogically sound word-based taxonomy will be a useful complement to the conventional structure-based taxonomy.

A survey of a number of relevant works on ESL errors, error analysis and crosslinguistic influence involving Hong Kong Chinese learners shows that these works fall into two main types:

(a)scholarly work appearing in journal articles, and

(b) books on common errors.

Most scholarly work in these areas appears in publications of academic departments of local universities, while specialist volumes on common errors are meant to be for reference of local learners and teachers of English who make up the main target readers.

Local Research on ESL Errors

Perhaps the most conspicuous attempt to explore local ESL errors systematically and to assess their impact on teaching and learning is to be found in the second special issue of Institute of Language in Education Journal (ILEJ) edited by David Bunton and Christopher Green. It contains seven papers covering a wide range of related issues, from

Bunton's study assessing the distinctiveness of Hong Kong-specific errors vis-a-vis errors obtained in an international error sample, to Green's survey of teachers' perceptions of 'error gravity', which has a direct bearing on the grading of student compositions.

Bunton's findings show that only 108 (or 26.7 percent) of the 404 Hong Kong errors as stated in his book are actually represented in the international sample, suggesting that the majority of the errors are distinct to Hong Kong Chinese ESL learners, of which the clearest examples are the lexical misselection, semantic mismatch and inappropriate collocation. Many other structural errors are compared in his study.

Four other studies in the ILEJ volume make reference to local ESL errors. Newbrook critiques a number of locally produced 'guides to English usage', most of which were written by Hong Kong Chinese. Chan analyses errors involving the misuse of transitive verbs and passive construction found in 156 compositions of Form 6 students, and concludes that these two types of errors are probably due to negative transfer from Cantonese. Sung adopts a cross-sectional design to elicit written English output from 30 students of varying proficiency levels.

The results seem to lend support to the hypotheses that

(a) typological transfer of topic-comment structure so commonly found in Chinese varieties is attested, especially those with lower proficiency of English, and

(b) learners with higher proficiency levels tend to produce sentences with subject-predicate structure in accordance with norms of standard English, suggesting an interlanguage continuum along which the topic-comment structure gradually gives way to the more normative subject-predicate structure of English as the learner progresses to a higher proficiency level.

The last of the four studies in the above-mentioned ILEJ volume is a follow-up study of Webster et al. Based on written work by students, interviews with students and a questionnaire survey with ESL teachers at the British Council, Webster et al. present local ESL errors at various levels: from morphology, lexis, syntax to discourse. In Webster & Lam, some of these issues are clarified and extended, and a few misused verbs such as suggest, help, change and send are included.

Of theoretical interest in these two papers is that the authors attribute the errors, though not exclusively, to mother-tongue influence, including the slightly odd warning found ubiquitously in public blaces apparently translated from Chinese: When there is afire, do not use the lift, where the use of when in standard English, according to the authors, would suggest that a tire, or even several fires, will take place at some in specified time later.

Elsewhere, Newbrook explores typical errors in relative clauses. Yip & Matthews present evidence of Hong Kong learners' avoidance if-and difficulties using-relative clauses, especially when oblique or genitive is involved. Green examines the overuse of topic-comment tructure in Hong Kong Chinese learners' English which is cited as evidence of typological transfer, resulting in 'discourse accent'. Comparing 'Hong Kong English' with Singapore English, Budge attributes Hong Kong students' failure to mark plural nouns with [s] in writing partly to Cantonese phonology, that is, the fact that Cantonese has no final [s] or final consonant clusters. The same reason probably accounts for the systematic omission of plural marking for English words ending with alveolar fricatives.

Lee addresses pedagogical issues such as when to correct learner errors and what types of errors should receive priority attention of the ESL reacher. Based on oral classroom data, Lee discusses different levels of errors, their relative teachability, and the need for corrective treatment in cases where 'error gravity' is high, as when intelligibility or communicability is at take. She also expresses doubt about he desirability of correcting high-frequency errors and argues that, other mings being equal, it is error type rather than error token that matters. Further, he queries the practicality of the general advice that errors which stigmatise he learner should be corrected. In her view, this advice may not be easy to follow since it is not immediately clear which error is stigmatised by which type(s) of native speakers.

More recently, there are a few corpus-based projects of ESL errors involving Chinese learners. Granger et al. report work in progress on their ICLE project (International Corpus of Learner English) involving learner errors from nine L1 backgrounds, including Chinese. From each of the nine sources, a computerised one-million-word corpus comprising written data of five different learner varieties will be created. Learner profile will be carefully controlled' to ensure comparability. Native-speaker language output will be used as baseline data for comparison. Data will be processed rigorously in five stages: encoding, mark-up, word-category tagging, parsing and coding.

In the same volume as Granger et al., McNeill gives a progress report of the development of a 'Hong Kong corpus of lexical errors in spontaneous speech' obtained from spontaneous conversations. He points out the pedagogical limitations of using concordancing to study learner errors in a corpus, especially with regard to second language vocabulary acquisition and argues that, in terms of insights into the nature of learner difficulties or explanations as to why errors occurred in the first place, it does not seem fruitful to compare the correct English of native speakers' baseline data with L2 learner errors in a corpus.

From both the practical point of view of providing useful suggestions for making pedagogically sound error-correction instruction, as well as the theoretical perspective of enlightening the international research community on Hong Kong CIL-specific crosslinguistic influence and interlanguage research, there is clearly a need for a large-scale, systematic study of Hong Kong-based learner errors with a view to yielding empirical findings in order to

(a) establish taxonomies of errors with regard to different proficiency levels,

(b) design and experiment with remedial materials continually with a view to helping learners overcome recurrent ESL errors, and

(c) report findings to the international research community about universal as well as unique features of Hong Kong CIL.

Handbooks on Common Errors

In addition to scholarly research findings on ESL errors in Hong Kong mentioned above, there exist quite a few book-length descriptions of common errors targeting learners and teachers of English as a second language, serving primarily as reference books or handbooks though some of which are open to criticisms ranging from inaccurate descriptive content to inadequate proofreading. All of these handbooks aim at raising the reader's awareness to common lexical problems.

One interesting feature is that sometimes the corresponding Chinese vocabulary items or structures are invoked for comparison in the explanation of the possible origin of the errors, suggesting that from the authors' perspective, knowledge of Chinese may have been the cause, at least partly, behind the error in question. With the exception of Tse and Yiu, all the other works are written in English.

Many of these handbooks on common errors have been reprinted once or twice, suggesting that there is a sizeable market for them. In the absence of any reader survey, however, it remains unclear how they are actually used and how useful they are perceived by readers, especially ESL learners eager to improve their English proficiency. These handbooks constitute one body of potentially useful reference and resource for researchers when designing remedial activities to tackle specific structural and lexical problems.

Though some of these popular handbooks show a sensitivity to learner needs and either adopt a thematic approach to organise the materials such as telephoning, sport, meals and restaurants or specify the typical context or register of the errors in question, most of them have a common feature in their design: Problematic words are listed alphabetically like the entries of a dictionary.

There is of course no harm indexing the structural problem in question by making a lexical entry based on the high-frequency exponent of the misused structure, as in the case of difficult in, but for fuller information it would be useful if the embedded structural anomaly is cross- adjectives, especially easy, hard, difficult, necessary, common, suitable, convenient, inconvenient, possible, probable, impossible and improbable. Students who have understood the rule should be able to point out that is wrong and should be rewritten as "It is difficult for us to...", whereas is perfectly acceptable.

Corpus-based research on Hong Kong-specific learner errors, with the ultimate objective of helping ESL teachers deliver quality error-correction feedback to their students collectively. One intermediate goal of top priority is to establish two complementary taxonomies of errors. This is because, to be maximally useful and informative to the reader-user, a conventional taxonomy of structural anomalies should be complemented by a word-based taxonomy of lexical problems. After being consolidated, all the errors in the two taxonomies should subsequently be cross-referenced where appropriate, and fed into one single volume and/or electronic database for users' convenient reference.

Two partial taxonomies based on available data were presented for exemplification, and the awareness-raising correction procedures of two erroneous structures were given for illustration. When establishing the two taxonomies, care should be taken to ensure that all structural and lexical anomalies be descriptively adequate, illustrated with typical examples and their corrections and, where appropriate, furnished with possible reasons contributing to their formation.

Detailed error-correction procedures of a subset of more or less 'teachable' structural anomalies, after being empirically tried out and field-tested taking into account the learner's proficiency level, should be written in a user-friendly manner, best separately listed and probably best presented in A-4 sheets coated or laminated in plastic in anticipation of durable use. It is important to field-test the error-correction procedures and to allow the test results to feed back into the design of the procedures, for this will help ensure that the proceduralised awareness-raising error-correction feedback be pedagogically sound, effective and user-friendly.

INTERGRATING FORMAL GRAMMARS IN ENGLISH TEACHING

Traditional grammar textbooks have serious drawbacks which concern both their content and the way it is presented to the student. The introduction of the notional syllabuses and the almost general adoption of the communicative approach have somehow changed the general attitude and the strategies utilised in foreign language teaching, but even the grammars that follow these methodologies do not overcome the most severe limitation of what we call the naive approach to the representation of linguistic knowledge, i.e., the incapacity to provide a global and coherent model of language.

The formal grammars developed by linguists, on the other hand, show their shortcomings when we try to use them directly for didactic purposes. The point is that these grammars have been developed to pursue goals that are different from those of school grammars. Theoretical linguists are in fact interested in providing mathematically well defined descriptions of a language which capture the competence of a native speaker. Computational linguists are interested in discovering computationally effective models of the processes that allow the speaker to utter or to understand a sentence in that language. Considered from the point of view of a foreign language teacher, these formal descriptions are generally useless since the (meta)language in which they are framed and the concepts which they are grounded upon are different from those utilised in daily teaching.

Systemic Approach

According to the systemic approach, two assumptions are made concerning the grammar of the English tense. These assumptions are:

— Tense opposition: the tense in English is considered as a three term opposition. From a linguistic point of view, it is an opposition of past vs. present vs. future; from a semantic point of view, as we will see below, it is interpretable as a precedence relation between two temporal variables.

— Seriality: complex tense combinations can be constructed by repeatedly selecting among the three term opposition.

As far as the first assumption is concerned, it should be noted that not all the linguists agree with the idea of English as a three-tense language. It is sometimes claimed, in fact, that in English it is possible to distinguish only between present and past, the future being a modal form of the present.

The second assumption reduces the process of tense selection to a series of iterative choices concerning the three term option. In other words, a tense combination like "is going to have built' is chosen by picking up the first time (primary tense) the present, then (secondary tense) the future and finally (ternary tense) the past. The name for a tense combination in the systemic approach is determined by considering the inverted order of the choices: in our case the tense combination is a past in future in present.

An important point concerns which possible tense combinations are allowed. It should be noted that, according to Halliday, up to quinary tenses (like: "will have been going to have been taking" : a present in past in future in past in past) are admissible in English.

The restrictions that the English grammar puts on the possible tense combinations are called 'stop rules' by Halliday and can thus be paraphrased:

— The present can occur only at the ends of the tense sequence (as a beginning or final choice).

— Except in the last and penultimate place, the same tense Cannot occur in two consecutive positions.

— The future can occur only once, apart from the last position.

These rules define whether a tense combination is legitimate but they do not indicate how a given tense combination is selected. To this end a significant contribution has been given by Matthiessen with his notion of chooser. To each option concerning the tense, and represented in the grammar through a system, Matthiessen assigns a chooser that states how the selection among the options specified is controlled. A chooser is a procedure that consists of steps that ascertain conceptual distinctions and make grammatical choices according to the conceptual distinctions.

According to this point of view, a verb tense essentially indicates the temporal relation which holds between the speaking time and the event time, and the tense selection process is determined by such a relation. More particularly, for each iteration step, the choosers take into account a relation of precedence (anteriority) - that we symbolize through "<' - between two different temporal variables (let us call them Tx and Ty) and:

— if Tx come after Ty (Ty < Tx), then the past is chosen;

— if Tx comes before Ty (Tx < Ty), then the future is chosen;

— if none of the above alternatives holds, then the chosen tense is present.

The process, in other words, starts by setting the time variable Tx to the speaking time Ts and by looking for the comparison time Tc, i.e., the time interval the speaking time is related to. This is the time that is assigned as a value to Ty. At this point it is possible to choose the primary tense according to the relation which holds between Tx (= Ts) and Ty (=Tc). If the comparison time matches the event time Te, then the temporal relation holding between Ts and Te has been found and the resulting tense combination consists only of a primary tense. If, on the other hand, the comparison time is different from the event time, the process cannot terminate since no temporal relationship has been established between the speaking time and the event time. A new iteration cycle starts by assigning the old Tc to Tx and by looking for a new comparison time Tc to be assigned to Ty.

The choice of the secondary tense is made again according to the relation holding between Tx and Ty and the process terminates if Tc matches Te. If this is not the case, the process goes on according to the same modalities with a tertiary, quaternary or quinary tense, until a link between the speaking time and the event time will be found.

Joining the Naive and Systemic Approaches

The view of grammar as a set of resources from which to choose, and the focus on the social role of language, are two of the reasons that support systemic grammar as a candidate formalism for didactic utilisation. It is evident, in fact, that the notion of choice, the concept on which such grammars are based, is more familiar to teachers and students than other abstract principles which other formalisms rely upon.

The emphasis on the functional organisation of the language - how it presents speakers with systems of meaningful options as a basis for communication - makes systemic grammar in keeping with modern approaches to language teaching. But there are other reasons that support such a choice. Among these we mention:

— the fact that the grammar of tense, the subset of language that concerns us in the ET project, is well documented in the systemic approach through papers by Halliday himself and, from a computational point of view, by Matthiessen;

— the interest shown by Halliday for the issues related to teaching, and the fact that much of his writing has been aimed at this topic;

— the fact that the systemic approach provides us not only with a static description of linguistic structures but, especially in the computational application of Matthiessen, with a runnable model of language;

— the fact that it is possible to translate the systemic approach into rigorously formal terms and to express it into a notation that is compatible with the formalisms, like functional unification grammar, currently used in computational linguistics.

For all these reasons, the systemic approach has been judged particularly suitable to serve as the conceptual ground for an intelligent tutoring system devoted to the foreign language teaching.

The most important problem that has been dealt with in applying the systemic model to the representation of the grammatical knowledge for the new Verb Generation expert has been that of the construction of the tense determination rules (choosers) capable of establishing in a cognitively transparent way a tense combination according to the assumptions of seriality and opposition of the systemic approach.

Solving the problem of tense determination according to the systemic approach requires finding the solution to the following subproblems:

— how to choose the tense in each iteration step;

— how to stop the iteration process.

We have examined in a previous section Matthiessen's proposal. His procedure for choosing the tense in each step is based on successive comparisons between the reference and the comparison time, while the termination procedure is based on a match between the current comparison time and the event time.

The burden of the whole process falls primarily on the identification, in each iteration step, of the appropriate comparison time. and this is performed through a dialogue between the choosers and an environment representing the semantic and pragmatic factors influencing the choice of the tense. These factors are, however, hidden from the choosers which simply receive from the environment the answers to their inquiries.

It is possible to make explicit the criteria underlying the determination of the tense and build eognitively adequate choosers that utilise them directly. In our new approach, this is done by dividing the features used by the tense selection rules of the naive grammar into two classes: the first class comprises those features which express the temporal relation among the time intervals occurring in the exercise sentence; the second class comprises the features of morphological, syntactic, semantic, and pragmatic information. These two classes play a different role in determining a tense combination. More particularly, the temporal features are utilised by a first type of chooser which discriminates in each iteration step between past vs. present vs. future.

The remaining features are utilised by a different category of choosers whose task is to establish whether the tense selection process should be iterated or not. The decision of the termination choosers is not based on a simple matching procedure which checks whether a link between the speaking time and the event time has already been established. This decision instead exploits a series of more complex factors through which the criteria underlying the determination of a tense combination in a given language are made explicit.

Let us clarify this new approach, which integrates the systemic treatment of tense with the use of the features found in the naive grammars, by reconsidering, as an example, the exercise presented in a previous section:

Yesterday, when I (arrive), Tom (talk) on the telephone.

The solution to this exercise requires the use of the (simple) past for the first verb and the present in past (or past continuous) for the second open item. While in the previous version of the Verb Generation Expert these solutions were chosen through appropriate rules that directly established the correct tenses, according to the systemic theory the tense determination process is iterative. In other words, the first tense is determined by choosing past for the primary tense and halting the process. The second tense is determined by choosing past as the primary tense, iterating the selection process for the secondary tense in which present is chosen, and then stopping.

In order to perform such a process, both the selection and termination choosers are needed. In our case, the following chooser applies:

IF *the clause describes a past event,*

the reference time is past,

THEN *set the primary tense to past.*

This chooser is very similar to the naive tense selection rule utilised to establish that a given verb should be conjugated into the simple past: it has been obtained, in fact, by withdrawing from that rule the condition concerning an aspectual feature. The selection choosers work thus by exploiting only the temporal features, and the choice among past vs. present vs. future is performed by taking into account only the temporal relations among the states and events described in the sentence. This chooser allows the identification of past as the primary tense for both the open items of the exercise. As for the first open item, after the primary tense has been selected, a termination chooser can be applied:

IF *the primary tense is past*

the clause contains an explicit time

expression the action described in the clause has been completed

THEN *stop.*

The termination choosers work by exploiting features of morphological, syntactic, semantic, and pragmatic information. While the tense selection choosers take into account the temporal aspects of the tense determination process, the termination choosers represent an interface between the tense system of a particular language and the relationships among the states or events described in a sentence the speaker intends to convey through the usage of a given tense.

The first condition determines the applicability of the chooser, while the remaining conditions put forward two of the criteria that establish when the simple past represents a necessary and sufficient tense combination for expressing a given meaning: i.e.. when the action described in the sentence has been completed in the past at a definite time.

No termination choosers are applicable to the second open item which therefore resorts to a secondary tense selection. The following selection chooser applies:

IF	*the clause has a definite reference time,*
	the event time is equal to or includes the reference time
THEN	*set the secondary tense to present.*

As a result of the action performed by the chooser, the secondary tense is set to the present. After the secondary tense has been determined, the following, very simple, termination chooser applies:

IF	*the primary tense is present, the secondary tense is past*
THEN	*stop.*

According to the systemic grammar of English tense, in fact, no further tenses are possible after a combination of present in past has been chosen.

Bibliography

Avery, P. & Ehrlich, S. *Teaching American-English Pronunciation*. Oxford: OUP. 1992.

Bailey, K.M., Long, M.H. & Peck, S. (eds.). *Second language acquisition studies*. Rowley, MA: Newbury House. 1983.

Bens, A. *Active English. Pronunciation and speech*. Englewood Cliffs, NJ: Prentice Hall Regents. 1977.

Bishop, W., *Released into language: Options for teaching creative writing*, Urbana, IL: NCTE, 1990.

Buehl, D., *Classroom strategies for interactive learning*, Schofield, WI: Wisconsin State Reading Association, 1995.

Burke, J., *Reading reminders: Tools, tips, and techniques*, Portsmouth, NH: Boynton/Cook, 2000.

Caplan, R., *Writers in training: A guide to developing a composition program for language arts teachers*, Palo Alto, CA: Dale Seymour, 1984.

Childers, P., Hobson, E. H., & Mullin, J. A., *ARTiculating: Teaching writing in a visual world*, Portsmouth, NH: Heinemann-Boynton/Cook, 1998.

Clarey, M.E. & Dixson, R.J. (1985). Pronunciation exercises in English. New York: Regents Publishing Company, Inc.

Collom, J., & Noethe, S., *Poetry everywhere: Teaching poetry writing in school and in the community*, New York: Teachers & Writers Collaborative, 2000.

Dean, D., *Strategic writing: The writing process and beyond in the secondary English classroom*, Urbana, IL: NCTE, 2006.

Dellinger, D. G., *Out of the heart: How to design writing assignments for high school courses*, Berkeley, CA: Bay Area Writing Project, 1982.

Golden, J., *Reading in the dark: Using film as a tool in the English classroom*, Urbana, IL: NCTE, 2001.

Jago, C., *Classics in the classroom: Designing accessible literature lessons*, Portsmouth, NH: Heinemann, 2004.

Johnsen, Julia E. *Basic English*. New York, The H.W. Wilson company, 1944

Kajder, S. B., *The tech-savvy English classroom*, Portland, ME: Stenhouse, 2003.

King-Shaver, B, & Hunter, A., "Differentiated instruction in the English classroom: Content, process, product, and assessment", Portsmouth, NH: Heinemann, 2003.

Noden, H., *Image grammar: Using grammatical structures to teach writing*, Portsmouth, NH: Heinemann, 1999.

Noguchi, R., *Grammar and the teaching of writing: Limits and possibilities*, Urbana, IL: NCTE, 1991.

Ogden, C. K . *The A B C of Basic English*. London, K. Paul,Trench, Trubner & Co. Ltd., 1932.

Richards, I. A . *English Through Pictures; a self-teaching way into English with directions in Spanish, French, Italian [and] German*. New York, Pocket books. 1950.

Shuman, R. B., & Wolfe, D., *Teaching English through the arts*, Urbana, IL: NCTE, 1990.

Smagorinsky, P., and others, *Explorations: Introductory activities for literature and composition*, Urbana, IL: ERIC/NCTE, 1987.

Wong, R. *Teaching Pronunciation: Focus on English Rhythm and Intonation*. Englewood Cliffs, NJ: Prentice Hall Regents. 1987.

Young, Art. *Writing Across the Curriculum*. Englewood Cliffs, NJ: Prentice-Hall, 1994.

Zinsser, William. *Writing to Learn*. New York: Harper & Row, 1988.

Index